Displays and Exhibits in College Libraries

CLIP Note #25

Compiled by

Jane Kemp
Luther College
Decorah, Iowa

Laura Witschi
Nevada State Library and Archives
Carson City, Nevada

College Library Information Packet Committee
College Libraries Section
Association of College and Research Libraries
A Division of the American Library Association
Chicago 1997

The paper used in this publication meets the minimum requirements of American National Standard for Information Sciences–Permanence of Paper for Printed Library Materials, ANSI Z39.48-1992. ∞

Library of Congress Cataloging-in-Publication Data
Kemp, Jane
    Displays and exhibits in college libraries / compiled by Jane
Kemp, Laura Witschi.
      p. cm. -- (CLIP note ; #25)
    Includes bibliographical references.
    ISBN 0-8389-7899-1 (alk. paper)
     1. Academic libraries--United States. 2. Library exhibits--United
States. I. Witschi, Laura. II. Title. III. Series: CLIP notes ;
#25.
Z675.U5K46 1997
027.7'074'73--dc21   97-18929

Printed on recycled paper.

Printed in the United States of America.

01 00 99 98 97   5 4 3 2 1

Table of Contents

INTRODUCTION

Humboldt State University Library
Humboldt State University
Arcata, CA

Roscoe L. West Library
Trenton State College
Trenton, NJ

Ida Jane Dacus Library
Winthrop University
Rock Hill, SC

Abell Library
Austin College
Sherman, TX

LeMoyne College Library
LeMoyne College
Syracuse, NY

Gregg-Graniteville Library
University of South Carolina
Aiken, SC

San Marcos Library
California State University
San Marcos, CA

Herrick Memorial Library
Alfred University
Alfred, NY

Oberlin College Library
Oberlin College
Oberlin, OH

Oesterle Library
North Central College
Naperville, IL

Thomas Byrne Memorial Library
Spring Hill College
Mobile, IL

Magale Library
Southern Arkansas University
Magnolia, AR

San Marcos Library
California State University
San Marcos, CA

Memorial Library
Berry College
Mount Berry, GA

Bowdoin College Library
Bowdoin College
Brunswick, ME

Upjohn Library
Kalamazoo College
Kalamazoo, MI

Livingston Lord Library
Moorhead State University
Moorhead, MN

D'Youville College Library
D'Youville College
Buffalo, NY

Sojourner Truth Library
State University of New York (SUNY)
New Paltz, NY

Courtright Memorial Library
Otterbein College
Westerville, OH

Sarah Byrd Askew Library
William Patterson College
Wayne, NJ

Connecticut College Library
Connecticut College
New London, CT

D'Youville College Library
D'Youville College
Buffalo, NY

Wolfgram Memorial Library (Photo)
Widener University
Chester, PA

Sojourner Truth Library
State University of New York (SUNY)
New Paltz, NY

San Marcos Library
California State University
San Marcos, CA

Oberlin College Library
Oberlin College
Oberlin, OH

Nyselius Library
Fairfield University
Fairfield, CT

Mabee Library
Washburn University
Topeka, KS

Boatwright Memorial Library
University of Richmond
Richmond, VA

Connecticut College Library (Photo)
Connecticut College
New London, CT

Smith College Libraries
Smith College
Northampton, MA

Ida Jane Dacus Library
Winthrop University
Rock Hill, SC

Reinsch Library
Marymount University
Arlington, VA

Emerson College Library (Photo)
Emerson College
Boston, MA

McCabe Library
Swarthmore College
Swarthmore, PA

Connecticut College Library
Connecticut College
New London, CT

David Bishop Skillman Library
Lafayette College
Easton, PA

Knight-Capron Library
Lynchburg College
Lynchburg, VA

Occidental College Library
Occidental College
Los Angeles, CA

D'Youville College Library (Photo)
D'Youville College
Buffalo, NY

Knight-Capton Library
Lynchburg College
Lynchburg, VA

Harry C. Trexler Library
Muhlenberg College
Allentown, PA

Connecticut College Library
Connecticut Library
New London, CT

Occidental College Library
Occidental College
Los Angeles, CA

Magale Library (Photo)
Southern Arkansas University
Magnolia, AR

Houghton Memorial Library (Photo)
Huntingdon College
Montgomery, AL

Sheean Library (Photo)
Illinois Wesleyan University
Bloomington, IL

Swisher Library and Learning Resource Center (Photo)
Bethune-Cookman College
Daytona Beach, FL

INTRODUCTION

OBJECTIVE

The *College Library Information Packet (CLIP) Notes* publishing program, under the auspices of the College Libraries section of the Association of College and Research Libraries, provides "college and small university libraries with state-of-the-art reviews and current documentation on library practices and procedures of relevance to them" (Morein 1985). This *CLIP Note* provides information on displays and exhibits in small college and university libraries.

Displays and exhibits have long been an accepted yet under-documented area of library work. This survey presents a collection of data and supporting documents about current display and exhibit practices in small-to-medium sized academic libraries. Goals were not only to examine whether the conclusions cited in the literature and the authors' experience were corroborated by survey evidence, but also to promote, through the specificity of questions, an understanding of the depth and significance of the subject. Since exhibit-related publishing in library literature usually focuses upon methodology rather than objectives, goals, management or academic value, the design of the survey was intended to prompt respondents to gain new perspectives when working with displays and exhibits.

BACKGROUND

The literature suggests that ambivalence (Bowen 1993) and lack of specialization or systematic planning (Tanasoca 1972) relegated a potentially powerful interpretive tool such as displays and exhibits to a "stepchild" role secondary to other core library activities (reference, cataloging, collection development, etc.). That library exhibit preparation remains largely an "illegitimate" activity (Bowen 1993) and has a nearly non-existent profile in the library profession is puzzling in light of the preponderance of exhibit facilities available and mounted within library buildings. The availability of exhibit facilities within academic libraries may be a relic of the past when there was a historically close relationship between libraries, museums and archives (Gundersheimer 1988), or, may be an expression of the philosophical desire for collection interpretation that is seldom realized since other library functions have been assigned a higher priority.

Although exhibits are assumed to be worthwhile (Caswell 1985), it is seldom that exhibition work appears in library budgets, job descriptions, library school course work, or professional training opportunities. It is also rare that exhibit work is viewed as a means of professional or faculty development. Although exhibits usually serve an educational or promotional role (Powers 1978, Caswell 1985), exhibit planning seldom results in recognition for their creation, despite the fact that exhibit work parallels the process of scholarly publishing (Bowen 1993).

SURVEY PROCEDURE

The authors used the standard procedure for *CLIP Notes* surveys. The initial proposal and draft of the questionnaire were submitted to the *CLIP Notes* Committee of ACRL's College Library Section and were reviewed and approved. Surveys were mailed to participants in April 1996 and returned through several months, concluding at the end of July 1996.

Surveys were sent to 260 college and university libraries. The institutions ranged in size from fewer than 1,000 students to over 6,000 students. While 24% of the respondents were public institutions, 76% were private. Collection size ranged from 50,000-100,000 to over 600,000 monograph titles with 101,000-200,000 being the mode (36%).

DISPLAYS AND EXHIBITS IN COLLEGE LIBRARIES

209 responses; 80% response rate. For purposes of survey analysis, "mode" is defined as the most frequent response.

Institution Name:
Address
Name of Respondent
Title
Work Telephone
E-mail address
Fax

1.   **Type of institution:**

All percentages based on 209 survey responses.

  49 Public   (24%)
156 Private (76%)
   4 Non responses

2.   **Staffing:**
Please provide the following information for the most recent fiscal year completed.

All percentages based on 209 survey responses.

    A.   **Number of FTE students:**
              Responses: 158
              Range: 600 - over 6,000
              Mode: 1,001-2,000 FTE students (31%)

    B.   **Number of FTE faculty:**
              Responses: 148
              Range: 26 - over 300
              Mode: 76-100 FTE faculty (14%)

    C.   **Number of FTE Librarians:**
              Responses: 169
              Range: 1-2 - over 13
              Mode: 4-6 FTE librarians (22%)

    D.   **Number of FTE library support staff:**
               Responses: 170
              Range: 1-2 - over 25
              Mode: 5-8 FTE library support staff (26%)

    E.   **Annual total of volunteer hours:**
              Responses: 149
              Range: 0 - over 1,500
              Mode: Zero volunteer hours (81% have zero volunteer hours)

3.   Size of collections
      Please provide the following information for the most recent fiscal year completed.

      A.   Number of monograph volumes in your library:
            Responses: 160
            Range: 50,000 - over 600,000
            Mode: 101,000 - 200,000 volumes (36%)

      B.   Number of monograph titles in your library:
            Responses: 121
            Range: 25,000 - over 400,000
            Mode: 101,000 - 150,000 monograph titles (19%)

4.   **Budget**
      Please provide the following information for the most recent fiscal year completed.

      All percentages based on 209 survey responses.

      A.   **Annual budget (include salaries)**
            Responses: 149
            Range: $201,000 - over $3,000,000
            Mode: $1,100,000 - $2,000,000 (32%)

      B.   **Annual budget (exclude salaries)**
            Responses: 110
            Range: $76,000 to over $2,000,000
            Mean: $575,000
            Mode: $451,000 - $500,000

5.   **Does your library regularly present displays and exhibits?**
      Please check the appropriate response.

      All percentages based on 209 survey responses.

      174   Yes   (83%)
       28   No   (17%)

6.   **How often does your library regularly present displays and exhibits?**
      Please check the range which is most applicable.

| | % of 209 | |
Responses	Survey Responses	Frequency
12	6%	Once or twice a year
49	23%	Three to five times a year
56	27%	Five to ten times a year
48	23%	Ten or more times a year
8	4%	Irregular

      173 responses
      Mode: Five to 10 times a year (27% of 209 survey responses)

7.   What is the length of time most displays and exhibits are shown in your library?
     Please check the appropriate response.

	Always	Often	Sometimes	Seldom	Never	Always + Often as % of total	Total
1-4 weeks	27	76	32	7	2	72%	144
5-8 weeks	5	57	52	19	4	45%	137
Each semester or term	11	12	34	24	33	20%	114
Annually	5	3	8	14	59	9%	89

8.   What amount of space is designated in your library for displays and exhibits?
     Please fill in the blank.

All percentages based on total responses to question.

   A.   **Display cases (how many)?**
        Responses: 163
        Range: 0 - over 10
        Mode: 2 display cases (35 responses, 21%)

   B.   **Easels (how many)?**
        Responses: 79
        Range: 0 - over 10
        Mode: 1 easel (29 responses, 37%)

   C.   **Walls (number of running feet)?**
        Responses: 71
        Range: Under 1' - over 201 feet
        Bimodal distribution: 1 mode at under 1' (8 responses, 11%); another mode at 36-40' (8 responses, 11%)

   D.   **Bulletin Boards (number of running feet)?**
        Responses: 95
        range: 0 - over 50'
        Mode: 1-5' (32 responses, 34%)

   E.   **Shelves designated for display (number of running feet)?**
        Responses: 61
        Range: 0 - over 200'
        Mode: 1-20' (29 responses, 48%)

   F.   **Floor (number of square feet)?**
        Responses: 43
        Range: 0 - over 601'
        Mode: 1-50' (14 responses, 33%)

   G.   **Other**
        Responses: 15
        Named units: Courtyard, panels, tables, dividers, cart, wall cases, walk-in display, glass walls, windows

9. **What safeguards are provided for your library display and exhibit facilities?**
    Please check all that apply.

Responses	% of 209 Survey Responses	Control
51	24%	Lighting control
31	15%	Humidity control
43	21%	Temperature control
10	5%	Chemical/particulate/pest intrusion control
147	70%	Security (e.g., locks, monitors, etc.)
10	5%	Other

Mode: Security (70% of 209 survey responses)

10. **What is the stated purpose for mounting exhibits at your library?**
    Please check all that apply.

Responses	% of 209 Survey Responses	Purpose
115	55%	Educate patrons about the library
153	73%	Educate patrons about special subjects
112	54%	Inform patrons about institutional events
38	18%	Inform patrons about community activities
89	43%	Inform patrons about faculty scholarships, activities and interests
141	67%	Publicize library collections
48	23%	Publicize institutional collections
48	23%	Supplement curriculum
61	29%	Develop aesthetic sense of patrons
107	51%	Provide aesthetic pleasure for patrons
75	36%	Encourage collaboration with other departments
117	56%	Decorate or enhance the library
43	21%	Fill empty display furniture or space
13	6%	Other (most comments related to student art displays and/or curatorship opportunities)

11. How often are the following subjects the focus of displays and exhibits in your library?
Please check appropriate response.

	Always	Often	Sometimes	Seldom	Never	Always + Often as % of total	Total
Academic disciplines	8	65	61	13	6	48%	153
Library interests	3	19	82	40	10	14%	154
Work of art/art-related	20	37	66	27	10	36%	160
Calendar events	2	66	63	12	12	44%	155
Current events	2	36	55	43	13	26%	149
Historical events	1	40	83	18	9	27%	151
Campus activities	7	47	68	23	10	35%	155
Community activities	0	12	24	63	43	8%	142
Famous individuals	1	23	90	33	10	15%	157
Geographic areas	0	7	51	62	26	5%	146
Ethnic groups	3	30	89	26	11	21%	159
Social concerns	0	15	59	54	20	10%	148
Curriculum supplementation	3	27	51	36	28	21%	145
Other	3	4	6	2	5	35%	20

12. **How often are the following types of materials exhibited from within your library collections?**
Please check the appropriate response.

	Always	Often	Sometimes	Seldom	Never	Always + Often as % of total	Total
Archives/manuscript collections	15	56	56	24	15	43%	166
Art collections	17	21	44	32	39	25%	153
Books							
Regular collection	34	70	47	13	3	62%	167
Rare books/special collections	9	44	62	29	16	33%	160
Alumni authors	5	25	61	42	27	19%	160
Faculty/staff authors	12	34	79	24	16	28%	165
Computer-related	0	13	34	53	50	9%	150
Government documents	6	8	33	47	61	9%	155
Media	0	15	34	57	42	10%	148
Objects	9	40	78	24	9	31%	160
Posters	15	37	64	23	15	34%	154
Other	3	1	1	1	9	27%	15

13. **How often does your library exhibit the following types of materials from outside the library but from within the institution?**

Please check the appropriate response.

	Always	Often	Sometimes	Seldom	Never	Always + Often as % of total	Total
Art works from campus	16	17	31	40	58	20%	162
Art works by students	9	25	53	33	44	21%	164
Art works by faculty	3	11	50	46	53	9%	163
Books from faoulty collections	2	6	35	56	65	5%	164
Literary/science exhibits	1	7	41	48	60	5%	157
Objects from campus collections	1	18	62	42	37	12%	160
Publicity for campus events	14	36	52	35	26	31%	163
Other	3	0	2	1	12	17%	18

14. How often does your library exhibit the following types of materials from off campus?
Please check the appropriate response.

	Always	Often	Sometimes	Seldom	Never	Always + Often as % of total	Total
Art works	4	18	28	46	63	14%	159
Books	2	4	35	41	77	4%	159
Posters or poster displays	4	9	34	56	58	8%	161
Media	1	1	13	42	99	1%	156
Objects	1	3	42	52	59	2%	157
Publicity for non-campus events	2	6	25	51	72	5%	156
Other	2	1	3	2	22	10%	30
			Total Seldom + Never = 740 (76%)				978

15. From what sources do off-campus displays and exhibits frequently originate?
Please check the appropriate response.

	Always	Often	Sometimes	Seldom	Never	Always + Often as % of total	Total
Other libraries	1	4	23	34	75	4%	137
Other educational institutions	1	7	24	34	68	6%	134
Museums	4	7	24	32	69	8%	136
Community agencies	1	9	34	42	49	7%	135
Government agencies	0	5	23	38	67	4%	133
Commercial sources	0	1	18	36	62	< 1%	117
Individuals	4	31	55	20	33	24%	143
Other	3	5	2	2	18	27%	30

16.   How are displays and exhibits publicized and by whom?
Please check all that apply for library personnel and other offices of your institution.

	Prepared By Library Staff (% of total)	Prepared By Other Campus Office (% of total)	Total	Percent of 209 survey responses
Annual schedule	37 (70%)	16 (30%)	53	25%
Bibliographies	54 (98%)	1 (2%)	55	26%
Brochures or flyers	59 (59%)	41 (41%)	100	48%
Catalogs or guides	26 (65%)	14 (35%)	40	19%
Photographs of the exhibit	17 (43%)	23 (58%)	40	19%
Posters	39 (61%)	25 (39%)	64	31%
Notices in campus news organs	108 (71%)	44 (29%)	152	73%
Articles for newspapers	51 (48%)	55 (52%)	106	51%
Articles for magazines	15 (39%)	23 (61%)	38	18%
Radio publicity	11 (35%)	20 (65%)	31	15%
Television publicity	9 (33%)	18 (67%)	27	13%
Reviews	4 (25%)	12 (75%)	16	8%
Internet or LAN	38 (76%)	12 (24%)	50	24%
Other	10 (72%)	4 (29%)	14	7%

17. How widely is the publicity distributed?
Please list appropriate letter(s) with type of publicity. Each type of publicity may receive several letters. (e.g., Annual Schedule A,B,C)

A-Within Library   **D-Within State**
B-Within institution   **E-Within region**
C-Within town or city limits   **F-Nationally**

Type of Publicity	Total Responses (as% of 209 survey responses)	Range	Mode (most frequent distribution as % of this publicity type total responses)	Mode (most frequent distribution as % of 209 survey responses)
Annual schedule	67 (32%)	A-F	Within library: 30 responses (45%)	14%
Bibliographies	82 (39%)	A-F	Within library: 38 responses (46%) Within institution: 38 responses (46%)	18% 18%
Brochures or flyers	184 (88%)	A-F	Within institution: 70 responses (38%)	33%
Catalogs or guides	93 (44%)	A-F	Within library: 28 responses (30%) Within institution: 28 responses (30%)	13% 13%
Photographs of the exhibit	59 (28%)	A-F	Within institution: 22 responses (37%)	11%
Posters	89 (43%)	A-F	Within institution: 41 responses (46%)	20%
Notices in campus news organs	209 (100%)	A-F	Within institution: 137 responses (61%)	66%
Articles for newspapers	179 (86%)	A-F	Within town or city: 58 responses (32%)	28%
Articles for magazines	59 (28%)	A-F	Within institution: 18 responses (31%)	9%
Radio publicity	56 (27%)	A-F	Within town or city: 22 responses (39%)	11%
Television publicity	56 (27%)	A-E	Within town or city: 19 responses (34%)	9%
Reviews	27 (13%)	A-E	Within institution: 8 responses (4%)	4%
Internet or LAN	74 (35%)	A-F	Within institution: 26 responses (35%)	12%
Other	18 (9%)	A-F	Within institution: 9 responses (50%)	4%

18. **What written management policies or procedures does your library have which guide the administration of displays or exhibits?**
   Please check all that apply.

Responses	% of 209 Survey Responses	Policy Type
122	58%	Library has no written management policies or procedures
18	9%	Objectives and/or development policies
11	5%	Incoming/outgoing loan policies
13	6%	Insurance regulations
3	1%	Maximum values allowed for materials shown
8	4%	Security requirements
7	3%	Rotation guidelines
9	4%	Preservation/disaster preparedness
13	6%	Policy relating to censorship or complaints
12	6%	Staff/faculty/committee responsibilities
8	4%	Evaluation or review mechanisms
6	3%	Budget allotments
1	4%	Transportation guidelines
10	5%	Other (comments included: institutional display policy, loan policy, exemption from liability policy)

19. **What forms does your library use for the management of displays and exhibits?**
   Please check all that apply.

Responses	Percent of 209 Survey Responses	Form Type
12	6%	Contracts
3	1%	Budget forms
7	3%	Condition report forms
8	4%	Insurance forms
11	5%	Loan forms
2	1%	Values forms
2	1%	Evaluation forms
2	1%	Statistics forms
14	7%	Other (included waiver of liability/responsibility; separation records to identify items moved from collections in log of exhibit contents; arrangement diagrams with list of labels; reservation form, schedule form)

20.   **Who is responsible for displays and exhibits in your library?**
      Please check the appropriate response.

      All percentages are based on 209 survey responses.

      A.   **No particular staff are assigned this responsibility**
           Responses: 22 (11%)

      B.   **One or more librarians**
           Responses: 134 (65%)
           Mode: Reference and public service librarians (31%)

           Top five librarian titles responsible for displays and exhibits:
           1. Reference and public service librarians: 42 responses (20%)
           2. Archivists: 17 responses (8%)
           3. Special collections librarians: 13 responses (6%)
           4. Circulation librarian: 11 responses (5%)
           5. Library director: 11 (5%)

      C.   **One or more support staff**
           Responses: 81 (39%)
           Mode: Circulation support staff (15%)

           Top five support staff position titles responsible for displays and exhibits:
           1. Support staff: 14 responses (7%)
           2. Circulation manager: 12 responses (6%)
           3. Student assistants: 9 responses (4%)
           4. Administrative assistants: 8 responses (4%)
           5. Director's secretary and/or special collections assistant (each): 6 responses (3%)

      D.   **Groups or committees**
           Responses: 14 (6%)

      E.   **8–Volunteers**
           Responses: 8 (4%)

      F.   **Other staffing arrangements**

           -Administrative staff (1 response)
           -Graduate assistant (1 response) and student assistants (14 responses)
           -Exhibits Coordinator (1 response)
           -Art Department professors, staff or students (5 responses)

21.   **Indicate which library staff members have this responsibility written into their position descriptions.**
      Please check all that apply.

Responses	Percent of 161 Question Responses	Staff Type
72	45%	Responsibility not included in library position descriptions
43	27%	Librarians
32	20%	Support staff
14	9%	Other (included: archivists, special collections librarians, graduate and student assistants, graphic artist)

22. **Who handles complaints about exhibits in your library?**
Please circle all that apply.

	Always	Often	Sometimes	Seldom	Never	Always + Often as % of total	Total
Display/exhibit preparator	22	9	25	8	8	43%	72
Library director	75	15	15	9	5	76%	119
College administrator	7	0	5	16	15	16%	43
Other	22	1	4	2	4	70%	33

Comments:
-No complaints ever (19 libraries)
-Complaints are very rare (3 libraries)

23. **What are typical annual expenditures for displays and exhibits in your library?**
Please check the amount range that is applicable.

	By Library	By Institution	For Exhibit Lease/Rentals
No funds expended	52	44	38
$1-$99	76	2	2
$100-$499	34	5	2
$500-$999	5	1	1
$1,000-$4,999	5	4	2
$5,000-$9,999	0	0	0
Over $10,000	0	1	0

24. **Are funds for displays and exhibits included in your library's budget as a separate line item?**
Please check the appropriate response.

Responses	% of 122 Question Responses	Answer
11	9%	Yes
111	91%	No

25.   Does your library pursue or utilize special funding (e.g., grants, gifts) in addition to the library's budget to present displays and exhibits?
       Please check the appropriate response.

Responses	% of 126 Question Responses	Answer
24	19%	Yes
102	81%	No

26.   If you answered "yes" to question 32, where are the special requests targeted?
       Please check the appropriate response.

	Always	Often	Sometimes	Seldom	Never	Always + Often as % of total	Total
Other offices within institution Please name the office: -Associated Students (often) -Each school awards grants (sometimes) -Academic departments (sometimes) -Alumni office (sometimes) -Special events (sometimes) -President, Dean of Faculty (seldom)	1	1	6	1	1	20%	10
Public granting agencies	0	2	2	4	2	20%	10
Private granting agencies	0	2	5	2	2	18%	11
Alumni	0	1	2	1	6	10%	10
Friends of the library	4	3	2	3	2	50%	14
Friends of the institution	1	2	1	0	4	38%	8
Other	1	0	0	0	1	50%	2

27. **Which of the following resources provided by the library or institution are available to staff performing display and exhibit functions?**
Please check all that apply.

Responses	% of 209 Survey Responses	Equipment
127	61%	Desktop publishing equipment
92	44%	Laminator
14	6%	Training in display/exhibit techniques or design
118	56%	Tools
84	40%	Workroom or non-public office preparation area
150	72%	Supplies (e.g., poster board, letter sets, signage kits, etc.)
154	74%	Display accessories (e.g., book supports, racks, cradles, etc.)
14	6%	Other (included: plasticades, dollies)

28. **What devices are most often used in your exhibits?**
Please check all that apply.

Device Type	Always	Often	Sometimes	Seldom	Never	Always + Often as % of total	Total
Explanatory labels	78	66	20	3	0	86%	167
Full-text narratives or inter.	5	32	63	32	15	25%	147
Objects	24	77	53	6	1	63%	161
Books or book jackets	49	77	34	3	1	77%	164
Media or media cases	7	24	49	56	14	21%	150
Photographs	10	86	67	5	0	57%	168
Credits/attribution/sponsor information	46	37	38	21	11	54%	153

29. **What access points or records does your library maintain on displays and exhibits?**
Please check all that apply.

27	**Bibliographic or archival-type record describing exhibit**	
	38	**Print format**
	4	**Electronic (in-house only)**
		3 **OPAC text display**
		0 **OPAC image display**
		1 **OPAC text and image display**
	3	**Electronic (shared)**
		5 **Campus LAN**
		2 **Remotely accessed via OPAC**
		0 **Bibliographic utility**
		1 **Exhibit record available via Internet**
7	**Electronic exhibit (includes surrogate image(s) of physical exhibit)**	
	10	**WWW Homepage access**
	2	**Graphics/audio/text markup or formats used**
		1 Print Shop/Adobe Photo

30. **In what format does your library prepare annual documentation about displays and exhibits in the library?**
Please check the appropriate response.

Responses	% of 209 Survey Responses	Form of Annual Documentation
93	44%	Library does not prepare annual documentation
11	50%	Annual report on displays and exhibits
52	25%	Summary on displays and exhibits included as part of library's annual report
14	7%	Other

31. **What auxiliary activities does your library use to supplement displays and exhibits?**
Please check the appropriate response.

Activity	Always	Often	Sometimes	Seldom	Never	Always + Often as % of total	Total
Gallery talks	0	7	23	16	86	5%	132
Receptions	7	14	36	30	55	15%	142
Workshops	0	1	8	25	92	<1%	126
Other	3	1	7	1	7	21%	19

32.   How would you improve displays and exhibits in your library?
Please circle the response on a scale of 1-5 with 1 being where most improvement is needed and 5 needing the least improvement.

	Scale of Improvement				
	Most Need	Some Need	Average Need	Little Need	Least Need
Rotate displays more frequently	11	19	34	25	53
Schedule displays for longer periods	1	7	13	31	80
Plan displays with more diverse content	11	40	33	28	26
Plan displays with more scholarly content	5	33	46	27	24
Plan displays with more popular content	3	24	47	29	26
Plan displays which more directly support curriculum	6	39	42	25	22
Improve environmental controls	36	34	17	26	24
Improve security	18	20	33	28	25
Improve preparation resources	31	37	38	26	6
Target more non-campus audiences	13	22	23	38	37
Increase off-campus publicity	18	28	31	24	35
Increase on-campus publicity	32	44	34	18	10
Acquire additional funding	34	35	38	19	13
Include responsibilities in position descriptions	15	23	29	30	39
Give scholarly/professional credit to preparators	11	18	38	24	39
Integrate displays and exhibits in library goals and objectives	21	23	32	37	21
Utilize viewer feedback/quality control mechanism	19	29	35	26	17
Other	7	4			

ANALYSIS OF SURVEY RESULTS

Frequency, Space, Safeguards and Purpose (Questions 5-10)

Displays and exhibits were regularly presented in the vast majority of responding libraries. There were no significant correlations between exhibit provision and/or frequency and the size of library budgets, number of professional or support staff members, or collection size. Survey results disclosed that the most popular exhibit rotation frequency among responding libraries was 5-10 times a year. However, popular frequency ranges spanned 3-10 or more times per year; such combined ranges were reported by the majority of all responding libraries. The most common length of time displays and exhibits were shown was 1-4 weeks. Surprisingly, given the apparent lack of formal support for exhibits, the least common length of time displays or exhibits were shown was annually. Only a few responding libraries reported permanent installations.

Most responding libraries had 1-3 display cases and 1-3 easels. Reported display and exhibit wall space ranged from under 1 running foot to over 201 running foot. The mode for bulletin board availability was 1-5 running feet, with a majority of reporting libraries having utilized 1-10 running feet of bulletin board space. Almost half of responding libraries reported between 1-20 running feet of shelves dedicated for displays or exhibits, while just over a third of reporting libraries had 1-50 square feet of available floor space for displays and exhibits, although nearly a quarter reported zero square feet for such purposes.

Probably because most libraries rely upon main library security as a default for display or exhibit security, "security" was the most utilized safeguard (70% of reporting libraries having used security in the form of locks, monitors, etc.) Lighting control for displays or exhibits was reported by nearly one quarter of responding libraries. However, other named exhibit security devices were seldom used. This is again indicative of the poor support display and exhibit activity has received in libraries.

Educating patrons about special subjects through displays or exhibits was very important to the great majority of academic libraries, suggesting widespread informal commitment to academic mission statements. More than half of responding libraries used displays or exhibits to publicize library collections and/or to educate patrons about the library, reflecting the academic library's commitment to bibliographic instruction. The practicality of the need to perhaps fill empty space was also suggested by the heavy response to "to decorate or enhance the library."

Subjects, Materials and Sources (Questions 11-15)

Displays and exhibits tend to focus on five major subject areas: academic disciplines, calendar events, works of art/art-related, campus activities, and, historical events. These results somewhat corroborate the results of Question 10 (relating to the purpose of displays and exhibits) discussed in the previous section. Perhaps because campus publicity and art works may have been readily available means of filling display areas, these items ranked high as subjects utilized. Academic discipline-related subject matter appears to be mostly prepared by library staff, with professorial subject specialists contributing only about one-fifth to one-quarter of those types of displays (see Question 12 results).

Popular materials utilized for displays and exhibits from within the library were: regular collection materials, archives/manuscript collections, posters, objects and faculty/staff authorship materials. The least popular library material for displays or exhibits was computer-related materials and government documents.

The most utilized library display or exhibit materials from outside the library but originating within the institution were publicity for campus events and art works. These results further suggest usage of readily-available materials to fill display/exhibit spaces. However, these materials categories resulted in many more responses of "seldom" or "never." For all materials categories there were 159 responses of "often" or "always" displayed, compared to 656 of "seldom" or "never." Thus, non-library campus sources were not highly utilized.

The most often used off-campus-originating materials utilized for library displays and exhibits were art works. However, 76% of responding libraries displayed off-campus materials "seldom" or "never." It seems clear that the surveyed libraries do not draw on external sources for exhibit materials. For the occasional utilization of off-campus display items, the mode are borrowed from individuals.

Publicity, Policies and Forms (Questions 16-19)

Notices in campus news publications ranked as the most utilized display and exhibit publicity vehicle. Not surprisingly, library staff rather than other campus offices prepared notices in campus news publications for most responding libraries.

Newspaper articles ranked second as a publicity medium, with publicity origination more evenly spread between the library and other campus offices. Brochures or flyers were the third-ranked publicity medium, again with a somewhat even spread of origination between library and other campus office staff. Posters were used in just over one-third of responding libraries, these being largely prepared by library staff. Display or exhibit-related bibliographies were prepared solely by library staff in nearly all responding libraries. Although Internet or LAN display/exhibit publicity was apparently utilized by nearly one in four responding libraries, the authors were never able to verify the usefulness of those results via Internet search to provided homepages.

Distribution of publicity for exhibits can range from solely within the library to national coverage. As noted above, the number one publicity vehicle was notices in campus news publications, with the modal type distribution being within the institution. The second-ranked publicity vehicle was newspaper articles, with the modal-type of distribution being within the community. For third-ranked brochures or flyers, the most frequent type of distribution was within the institution.

Of responding libraries, 122 indicated they had no written display/exhibit management policies or procedures; 87 libraries failed to respond to this question. This poor response suggests that at the very least, over half of the libraries lacked any written policies or procedures. Objectives and/or development policies were the most common policy reported, but available in only one of ten reporting libraries. It appears that at best only a handful of responding libraries used any particular named form for the management of displays and exhibits. However, the preponderance of non- responses to each of these named forms (averaging 202 out of 209 possible responses) renders these results almost unusable.

Staffing (Questions 20-22)

The responsibility for managing displays and exhibits has been largely assigned to librarians, although support staff were also assigned the task, sometimes in tandem with the librarian. At 11% of the responding libraries, no particular staff were designated as responsible, while groups/committees were responsible in even fewer of the institutions. Among librarians, reference or public services librarians were most frequently assigned these tasks, while librarians who were archivists and special collections librarians also managed displays and exhibits. Among support staff, circulation managers were most often given this responsibility. Remaining support staff listed ranged among 20 specified staff titles. The number of groups/committees or volunteers who were responsible for these tasks was marginal. Other staffing arrangements included a variety of titles, with student assistants mentioned most frequently. Percentages of the particular positions involved were so inconsistently applied that summary statements about them could not be compiled.

It is significant that 45% of libraries responding reported that these responsibilities were not included in library position descriptions. Thus, these responsibilities were formally assigned in almost one-half of the responding libraries. Where responsibilities were assigned, respondents reported they were in the position descriptions of librarians more often than in those of support staff, although the percentages were not far apart.

Complaints about displays and exhibits were handled overwhelmingly by library directors, followed by display/exhibit preparators and college administrators. It should be noted that twenty-two respondents commented they rarely or never had received complaints.

Funding (Questions 23-26)

No funds were expended on displays and exhibits by the library in 30% of the responding libraries. Where the library was the agency which supplied funds, over half of the respondents reported funding under $99, while less than 10% were over $500. Where the institution was the funding source, 77% of responding libraries reported no funds were expended. The remaining libraries reported that funding was spread fairly evenly among the categories. Exhibit lease/rentals were not funded in 84% of the responding libraries.

Funds for displays and exhibits were included as a separate line item in only 9% of responding libraries. Special funding was sought at only 19% of responding libraries. The few special requests made were targeted to a range of departments within and outside the institution with no particular group receiving attention. Clearly, funds for displays and exhibits in academic libraries are meager at most colleges.

Miscellaneous (Questions 27-32)

Resources provided by the library or institution were available in over half of the responding libraries with display accessories, supplies, desktop publishing equipment, and tools receiving the highest responses. Training in display/exhibit techniques or design was available in only 6% of responding libraries or institutions.

Devices most often used in displays and exhibits, were explanatory labels, books or book jackets, objects, photographs, and credits. Full-text narratives and media were used much less frequently.

Access points or records maintained by libraries on displays and exhibits were mostly in print format, although the number of responses to this question was very low. Only 5% of responding libraries indicated they had World Wide Web access to their displays and exhibits, with six providing site addresses.

Annual documentation on displays and exhibits was not prepared in almost half of responding libraries. Of those that did prepare such documentation, 25% included a summary of displays and exhibits as part of the library's annual report, while only 5% prepared a separate annual report devoted solely to displays and exhibits. Five comments indicated that displays and exhibits were included as part of the annual report of a particular library department.

Auxiliary activities were not often used by libraries to supplement displays and exhibits. Responding libraries reported such activities as workshops, gallery talks, or receptions were generally not utilized. Comments echoed this pattern.

Finally, displays and exhibits were seen by respondents as needing most improvement in the areas of increasing on-campus publicity, improving environmental controls, acquiring additional funding, and improving preparation resources. Areas needing the least improvement in the opinions of the respondents were scheduling displays for longer periods, rotating displays more frequently, targeting more non-campus audiences, and including responsibilities in position descriptions. Respondents commented that additional staff, time and funds were most needed to improve displays and exhibits.

CONCLUSION

While the overwhelming number of respondents replied that their libraries presented displays and exhibits (83%), the evidence indicates that these responsibilities were informally handled in most libraries. Most libraries did not create forms to manage the tasks and over half the libraries had no written management policies or procedures. Although resources such as space, some funding, supplies, equipment, and security were readily provided by most libraries, time for staff to produce displays and exhibits was scant. Survey respondents' comments indicated that display and exhibit responsibilities were often assigned by default to staff members who showed an interest in or flair for doing the work. Publicity was produced by many libraries for displays and exhibits, but few respondents provided auxiliary activities to supplement the event.

The place of displays and exhibits in academic libraries is accurately portrayed in the literature. While most libraries engage in the activity, most respondents reported they felt little need to improve displays and exhibits in significant ways such as boosting the status of the activity within the library structure or providing more credit or time to staff preparators. Thus, while the activity is common, recognition of its potential significance as an educational function of the library is lacking. Development of new attitudes toward displays and exhibits will be a challenge, but could change with inclusion of relevant coursework in library studies curriculums. Attitudes also might improve as movement toward library involvement in cyberspace is increased. The growing interest and availability of graphical Internet hyperlinks is cited as a powerful opportunity to provide exhibit-related scholarly output (O'Conner, 1996).

Library specialties have evolved with contemporaneous technology and user need (Tanasoca 1972). Online exhibits can be readily viewed on the World Wide Web, and indeed may lend themselves well to leading a remote user to hyper-linked bibliographic inquiry.

> Librarians should understand that what they do is create space, cognitive space in the environment. It can look like a public library, a Web site ... or whatever. Librarians need to make sure that they provide a rich space where human beings can gather, interact, and become more than themselves (Chepesiuk 1996).

Once the "virtual library" takes its place along with the traditional ordering of knowledge, librarians may assume interpretive and multi-media oriented roles. Librarians as "knowledge curators" could employ multi-media exhibit capabilities to impose value, order, or new concepts on information in all its available forms.

SELECTIVE BIBLIOGRAPHY

SELECTIVE BIBLIOGRAPHY

Books:

Dudley, Dorothy. *Museum Registration Methods*. 3rd ed. Washington, D.C.: American Association of Museums, 1979. NOTE: The 4th edition of this work is due in late 1997.

Everhart, Nancy. *Library Displays*. Metuchen, NJ: Scarecrow Press, 1989.

Malaro, Marie C. *A Legal Primer on Managing Museum Collections*. Washington, D.C.: Smithsonian Institution Press, 1985.

Perry, Kenneth D. *The Museums Forms Book*. rev. ed. Austin, TX: Texas Museums Association, 1990.

Richard, Mervin, et al. *Art in Transit: Handbook for Packing and Transporting Paintings*. Washington, D.C.: National Gallery of Art, 1991.

Serrell, Beverly. *Exhibit Labels: An Interpretive Approach*. Walnut Creek, CA: Alta Mira Press, 1996.

Schaeffer, Mark. *Library Displays Handbook*. New York: H.W. Wilson, 1991.

Stone, Charles A. *Charnell's Guide to Affordable Exhibits and Programs*. Little Falls, MN: Charnell, 1990.

Tedeschi, Ann C. *Book Displays: A Library Handbook*. Ft. Atkinson, WI: Highsmith Press, 1997.

Witteborg, Lothar P. *Good Show! A Practical Guide for Temporary Exhibitions*. 2nd ed. Washington, D.C.: Smithsonian Institution, 1991.

Wyly, Mary. *SPEC Kit: Exhibits in ARL Libraries*. SPEC Kit. 120. Washington, D.C.: Association of Research Libraries, 1986.

Articles

Allyn, Shawn A. And Gail F. Stern. "Using Archival Materials Effectively in Museum Exhibitions." *The American Archivist* 50 (Summer 1987): 402-404.

Avens, Irene. "On Running a Small Art Gallery in an Academic Library." *Art Documentation* 6 (Fall 1987): 121-123.

Bowen, Laurel G. and Peter J. Roberts. "Exhibits: Illegitimate Children of Academic Libraries?" *College & Research Libraries* 54 (September 1993): 407-15.

Bukoff, Ronald N. "Censorship and the American College Library." *College and Research Libraries* 56 (September 1995): 395-403.

Caswell, Lucy S. "Building a Strategy for Academic Library Exhibits." *College and Research Libraries News* 46 (April 1985): 165-168.

Chepesiuk, Ron. "Librarians as Cyberspace Guerrillas." *American Libraries* 27 (8): 49-51.

Gundersheimer, Werner. "Two Noble Kinsmen: Libraries and Museums." *Rare Books and Manuscripts Librarianship* 3 (Fall 1988): 91-101.

Hinson, Karen. "Exhibitions in Libraries: A Practical Guide." *Art Documentation* 4 (Spring 1985): 5-6.

Jones, Dorothy E. and Mary Grosch. "Exhibits Speak Louder Than Words." *Technicalities* 7 (September 1987): 6-8.

Kemp, Jane. "Creating Exhibits in the Academic Library." *College and Research Libraries News* 46 (July/August 1985): 162-166.

Morein, P. Grady. "What Is A *Clip Note*?" *College and Research Libraries News* 46 (1985): 226-229.

O'Connor, Diane Vogt. "Exhibitions in Cyberspace: Museum Documentation at the Millenium." *Art Documentation* 15 (1): 17-19.

Powers, Sandra. "Why Exhibit? The Risks Versus the Benefits." *American Archivist* 41 (July 1978): 302.

Simor, Suzanna. "Art Exhibitions in Academic Libraries: A Necessary (?) Luxury (?)." *Art Documentation* 10 (Fall 1991): 137-139.

Tanasoca, Donald. "Exhibits, Library." *Encyclopedia of Library and Information Science* 8 (1972): 289-296.

Wolf, Lisa F. and Jeffrey K. Smith. "What Makes Museum Labels Legible?" *Curator* 36 (2): 95-110.

Publications of Professional Organizations:

Publications of these organizations are uniformly excellent to consult when planning and preparing displays and exhibits. Both publish catalogs.

> American Association for State and Local History
> 530 Church Street, Suite 600
> Nashville, TN 37219

> American Association of Museums
> 1225 Eye Street, N.W., Suite 200
> Washington, D.C. 20005

To subscribe to an electronic list on library exhibits:

> Exhibits and Displays in Libraries
> list name: LIBEX-L
> send message to subscribe:
> "Subscribe LIBEX-L your name" to
> LIBEX-L@MAINE@NU021140@NDSUVM1
> address: NU021140@NDSUVM1

DOCUMENTS

SELECTION OF DOCUMENTS

Documents received from responding libraries for inclusion in the *CLIP Note* reflected the survey results. Most documents received were copies of policies and procedures which libraries used when planning displays and exhibits. Position descriptions submitted were for professional librarians, paraprofessionals or support staff positions in which display and exhibit responsibilities were considered a small portion of a position. No documents were received for a full-time position within a library for a person whose major or sole responsibility was for arranging displays and exhibits. The few annual reports submitted were for libraries where displays and exhibits were mentioned within the library's annual report or departmental reports. Mission statements received did not focus specifically on displays and exhibits but contained general wording about promoting library usage; thus, none were included among the documents portion of the *CLIP Note*.

Forms submitted from responding libraries also reflected the survey results. Although not all forms submitted could be used, the total number received was close to the number published. Clearly, since most of the responding libraries present displays and exhibits, the low number of forms received indicates academic libraries approach the activity in an informal manner.

Publications prepared by libraries indicate that, while they may manage displays and exhibits in an informal manner, they are active in publicizing them. A wide variety of publications were received, most professional in appearance.

Finally, it should be noted that this was the first *CLIP Note* which actively sought photographs of displays and exhibits. These were interspersed throughout the documents section to highlight particular documents and forms or to illustrate the type and format of displays and exhibits most typically prepared by libraries.

POLICIES
AND
PROCEDURES

EXHIBITS POLICY

1. **Policy**

   1.1. As used in this policy, "exhibits" includes collections of artifacts brought together in the Library's exhibit cases and other display facilities (i.e., designated wall space) exclusive of bulletin boards.

   1.2. In furthering its educational mission, HSU Library maintains a program of exhibits and displays.

   1.3. Exhibits may include artifacts of any kind on any subject which will be of general educational or cultural interest to the university community. The following types of exhibits will be particularly encouraged.

       1.3.1 Exhibits pertaining to major events on campus or in the community.

       1.3.2 Exhibits which assist members of the university community in understanding and making use of library, university, and community resources or of special relevance to the Library's collections and services.

       1.3.3 Exhibits which bring to members of the university community outstanding representatives of cultural or social phenomena not otherwise readily available in this community.

       1.3.4 Exhibits of work of artists, craftspeople, and the like.

   1.4. The content and workmanship of exhibits should be of good quality, in keeping with the Library's educational and cultural mission.

   1.5. The Library may solicit and encourage exhibits from any source within or outside of the university community, provided that, in the judgment of those in charge of the exhibits program, the material and manner of presentation meet the criteria set forth above.

2. **Procedures**

   2.1. The Library Administration staff is in charge of the exhibits program. An application will be provided to each individual or club at the time the reservation is made which outlines the rules and standards governing exhibits in the Library. The Library does not insure exhibits.

   2.2. Duties of the Administration staff are:

       2.2.1 To maintain a written schedule of exhibits and other necessary records.

       2.2.2 To supervise the mounting and dismounting of exhibits. The staff will provide the necessary hardware (i.e., hanging rods, book stands, etc.).

   2.3. Exhibits covered by this policy will be mounted in the Library building. Place and manner of mounting will be arranged to provide necessary security as well as desirable public exposure.

Reviewed via the Day File, 7-18-91

RULES AND STANDARDS GOVERNING EXHIBITS IN THE LIBRARY

POLICY

In furthering its educational mission, HSU Library maintains a program of exhibits and displays.

The content and workmanship of exhibits should be of good quality, in keeping with the Library's educational and cultural mission.

PROCEDURES

Within each exhibit case or designated wall space, there must be a card identifying the exhibitor and exhibit.

A special putty will be provided for mounting descriptive cards to the walls. (Tape is not to be used.)

If the large, fixed glass display case is used, the entire case must be utilized. A description of the exhibit is to be displayed in the glass frame mounted on the wall. (Nails are NOT to be used in the case; posters, pictures, etc., are NOT to be taped to the glass--straight pins will be provided upon request.)

We have several metal and one acrylic book display stand. Also, we will provide straight pins (nails are not to be used).

No electrical machines or appliances, such as slide or film projectors, may be used due to fire hazard.

No food may be used as part of an exhibit.

THE LIBRARY IS NOT RESPONSIBLE FOR DAMAGE TO OR THEFT OF EXHIBITS.

dlw
10/6/93 (rev.)

LIBRARY EXHIBIT POLICY

Campus individuals and groups are encouraged to use the library's locked exhibit cases to mount their own exhibits. To protect the exhibited items, to assure the best possible exhibits, and to limit the Library's obligation to a manageable level, the following policy governs library exhibits:

1)
Each exhibit must have at least one faculty/staff sponsor, who will:
        a) Discuss the exhibit with the librarian who will serve as the library liaison to the exhibit. (In most cases, this will be the appropriate Library subject specialist, but when the exhibit does not clearly fall into anyone's area of expertise, or when the appropriate librarian is overburdened, another librarian may be designated.)
        b) Work with the individual or group which is mounting the exhibit to assure that it is of acceptable quality and does not raise unanswerable concerns about content (e.g., an exhibit about neo-Nazis might be suitable, but an exhibit expressly celebrating neo-Nazis wouldn't be). Take responsibility for the content if it generates criticisms or protests.
        c) Provide a comprehensive prospectus indicating what the exhibit will look like --- e.g., signage, title, materials to be used, layout, etc.
        d) Provide the library with an itemized list, including a dollar value for each item, of every item to be exhibited. If an item has no value, please mark it on the list as "no value".
        e) Be sure that the necessary people are available to mount the exhibit at the designated time.
        f) Serve as the library's contact person for all technical problems ---e.g., arrange for any support needed to mount the exhibit, and be sure that it goes up and comes down on the agreed-upon dates. These tasks can be delegated, but the faculty/staff member is responsible if the delegated person does not follow through.
        g) Promote the exhibit by sending notification to the appropriate college publications (and beyond, if appropriate).

2)
In most cases, the library exhibit will include at least a few books on the subject that are owned by the library. The library liaison will work out with the faculty sponsor who will take responsibility for choosing the books. In some cases, it will probably be the librarian, in some cases the faculty sponsor, and in some cases the individual or group mounting the exhibit.

3)
Library staff will:
        a) Receive requests for exhibits.
        b) Arrange dates when the exhibits will go up and come down; register these on a special exhibits calendar and send a

follow-up note to the faculty sponsor. Exhibits will be scheduled on a first-come, first-served basis. In general, exhibits will stay up for about six weeks. Exhibits put up during May and December will stay up for the semester breaks.

    c) Identify a likely library liaison and convey the request to him/her through his/her supervisor.

    d) Complete and send the required insurance form, using the itemized list provided by the faculty sponsor one week before the exhibit is mounted.

    e) Check the completed exhibit to make sure that it conforms reasonably closely to the conspectus and is of acceptable quality. Contact the faculty sponsor if it does not or is not.

    f) Check the exhibit regularly to make sure that it is still in good shape, to make sure that it is not falling down, and notify the faculty sponsor if there are any problems.

    g) Call the faculty sponsor on the day that the exhibit is scheduled to be mounted --- if no one has shown up to mount it; and call the faculty sponsor on the day it is scheduled to come down --- if no one has shown up to take it down.

    h) Consult with the faculty sponsor and the individual or group mounting the exhibit on content, books to be included, etc.

Provisos:

1) The library is not responsible for the accuracy or tastefulness of the exhibits. However, the Library reserves the right to refuse to host an exhibit for any reason.

2) The library takes no responsiblity for the security of the exhibited items.

3) The Library takes no responsibility for the security of exhibited items that are left in the Library after the date on which the exhibit is scheduled to close or before the date it is scheduled to go up.

3) The Library does not have an exhibit staff. The exhibit contact person is Bridget Konkle, and she can be reached at X2574 for the scheduling of exhibits. On occasion, regular or student Library staff members may lend a hand, but this is not to be expected. The faculty/staff sponsor must be sure that sufficient workers are available to mount and remove the exhibit.

4) The Library cannot provide supplies or tools.

EXHIBITS COMMITTEE GUIDELINES

PURPOSE OF DACUS LIBRARY EXHIBITS

Exhibits will be used to increase student, staff, and faculty awareness of library holdings, services, and events; to educate patrons on the use of the library and its facilities; to highlight special holidays or calendar events of local or national importance, especially as they relate to library resources; and in general to entertain and to enlighten patrons.

COMMITTEE

The Exhibits Committee's primary role is to coordinate exhibits in the library. The committee recommends 5 members: 2 from TS, 2 from PS (including 1 representative from Archives/Special Collections), and 1 at large. Members are appointed by the Dean of the Library each July 1st. The committee members select/elect their chair each year; a vice-chair will handle problems in the chair's absence. The chair is responsible for submitting supply requests to the library administration, establishing the schedule of exhibits with other committee members, and handling any special difficulties which may arise. The chair should develop a budget based on need and availability of funds. The committee should make suggestions for supplies with the final decision left to the chair/vice chair.

SCHEDULING

The committee will accept applications from potential exhibitors three times a year: immediately before fall semester, spring semester, and summer session. These times will be publicized to the Winthrop community in alumni publications, F.Y.I. and the Johnsonian. Exhibit schedules will then be selected and scheduled one semester at a time by the committee as a whole. (See policies and criteria established below.) The schedule will be presented to the Dean of the Library for final approval. Additional applications throughout the semester will be considered only if a vacancy in the schedule permits. The chair is ultimately responsible for any changes in the schedule; input of the committee should be solicited when appropriate. One committee member will be assigned to each exhibit when the schedule is formalized. It is this committee member's responsibility to see that the exhibit is publicized, assembled, displayed, and disassembled in a timely manner, in accordance with the guidelines established. Exhibits will be displayed for no less than two weeks and no more than four weeks.

CRITERIA FOR SELECTION OF EXHIBITS
Applications will be reviewed by the following criteria, in order of importance:

1. Does it in some way relate to Dacus Library? (Will resources at Dacus be utilized?)

2. Is it Winthrop or higher education related?

3. Is it a subject of local importance? (ie: Come See Me, etc.)

4. Is the organization requesting exhibit space a service organization or a social organization according to their charter? Consideration will be given only to service organizations.

5. Is the size and nature of the display appropriate for the library? Exhibits of a controversial nature will not be avoided, but must be mounted with an awareness that opposing viewpoints should be afforded an opportunity for expression.

EXTERNAL REQUESTS

No individual or group (either internal or external to the university) will be guaranteed exhibit privileges for any specific time. Community groups will be allowed to exhibit materials only if the schedule permits; all applications will be considered by the committee in accordance with the criteria above. The library retains authority over size, nature, length, and date of display.

RESPONSIBILITY OF EXHIBITOR

The library will not be able to assume the responsibility for exhibit material that is lost, damaged, or stolen. Outside exhibitors should arrange for insurance if there are objects of significant value on display. The individual or group requesting exhibit space is responsible for transporting, displaying, maintaining, and dismantling all exhibit materials. All exhibits will be mounted, labeled, and displayed in a manner that reflects well on the library from a technical and professional standpoint.

PUBLICITY

Committee members should divide publicity work on an exhibit by exhibit basis, as specified above (see SCHEDULING). Publicity should carefully reflect the nature, significance, and dates of the exhibit. Exhibits of community interest should be publicized in both local and campus publications. Exhibits primarily related to Winthrop need only be published in Winthrop publications. The committee recommends that a press release be sent to appropriate papers (e.g. The Herald, The York Observer, The Johnsonian, and F.Y.I.) for 4 week exhibits and/or exhibits of major importance, such as traveling exhibits. Remember that press releases must be cleared by University Relations; allow plenty of time. Brochures/mailers may also be used to publicize the exhibit schedule at the committee's discretion. Furthermore, the committee may wish to be listed on various organizations' calendars for certain exhibits. (E.g. The local Commission on Women puts out a calendar of events for Women's History Month.)

SPACE UTILIZATION

No cases will be reserved permanently for any area of the library, but it is anticipated as a matter of course that the display cases immediately outside the Archives area will normally be devoted to Archives.

TRAVELING EXHIBITS

From time to time traveling exhibits are made available to the library. The Exhibits Committee will be solely responsible for selecting and obtaining appropriate exhibits of this type, and will give special consideration to those that are free of charge.

Abell Library Center
Exhibits Policy[1]

INTRODUCTION AND PURPOSE

Exhibits should reflect the scholarly, historical, social, and cultural concerns of Austin College and its community. Exhibits should focus on topics consistent with the overall scholarly and cultural concerns of Austin College.

This policy applies to the common areas, such as lobbies, foyers, corridors, general traffic areas, and study areas.

I. EXHIBIT GOALS

In general, the Abell Library Center's exhibit program's goals are:

A. To educate, enlighten and enrich through such means, the college community and the public;

B. To broaden the appeal of the library and the college to the public by increasing awareness of scholarly, historical, social, and cultural concerns.

Attainment of these goals is not easily measured. The constant flow of viewers may remain reason enough to continue this program.

II. LIBRARY EXHIBITS COMMITTEE

The Library Exhibits Committee consists of librarians and other members of the Abell Center Library staff as designated by the College Librarian. The Committee will work with exhibitors and will review all exhibit proposals. Recommendations will be made to the College Librarian regarding approval and scheduling. The Exhibits Committee may request that changes be made in the interest of aesthetics, content, preservation of materials, and general appropriateness to the Library and Austin College. Questions or problems concerning exhibits in the Abell library should be directed to the College Librarian. Further review may be required of the Library Exhibits Committee. Should the policy need further definition or should exceptions be requested, the College Librarian will exercise final authority, within the library, regarding interpretations and/or implementation. A member of the Library Exhibits Committee may be assigned to work with the exhibitor(s).

III. EXHIBIT GUIDELINES

A. FOCUS OF EXHIBITS

1. Exhibits will focus on topics consistent with the overall scholarly and cultural concerns of Austin College.

2. Exhibits are not be used to promote commercial concerns.

3. Exhibits that might be viewed as promoting personal or organizational concerns should be consistent with the overall scholarly and cultural concerns of Austin College.

4. Topics subject to controversy may and should be presented, provided that they are handled in an objective manner and are consistent with the overall scholarly and cultural concerns of Austin College. In this regard, the College Librarian will exercise final authority, within the library.

B. APPLICATION AND PRESENTATION

1. Application forms must be secured from the College Librarian or an individual designated by him/her, and returned to the College Librarian. While there is no firm deadline for proposals, all other factors being reasonably equal, priority will be given to the earliest proposal turned in to the College Librarian.

2. The proposal should try to achieve the best aesthetic and intellectual presentation possible consistent with the guidelines.

C. PRESERVATION GUIDELINES

The Abell Library Center has a responsibility to exhibit a broad range of library and related materials, including rare and valuable items from its collections, for the education and pleasure of the academic community. At the same time, the Abell Library is responsible for protecting and preserving these materials. The following guidelines are intended to allow the Library to fulfill both responsibilities. Sections 1 and 2 below apply primarily to the materials at Austin College under the care of the Abell Library Center.

1. Condition of Materials to be exhibited:

   a) The condition of exhibited materials directly reflects on the Abell library and its curatorial responsibilities. Consequently, exhibited materials should be in good condition as ascertained by the College Librarian or his/her designated representative. Condition Review must be requested as soon as possible to allow the exhibitor to choose alternative materials in better condition or to take other appropriate action. It is the responsibility of the exhibitor to request this review. Permission to exhibit materials may be denied at any time by the College Librarian if the materials are not in good condition or cannot be adequately protected.

   b) Very fragile, rare, unique, or otherwise extremely vulnerable materials should not be exhibited unless special arrangements are made with the College Librarian. In general, original photographs should not be exhibited unless special arrangements can be made. The Library cannot be held responsible for the loss or mutilation of exhibited materials.

2. Environmental Standards

   a) While reasonable care will be taken regarding environmental standards, exhibitors should be aware that materials may be subject to less than desirable environmental standards.

   b) The College Librarian or his/her designated representative will make the final determination regarding the adequacy of environmental standards for any library materials considered for display.

   c) Materials will not be displayed when doing so may have the effect of accelerating their deterioration or damaging other materials.

3. Manner of Exhibit

   a) Handling and Physical Support:
   Materials should be handled as little as is necessary in preparation and dismantling of exhibits. Physical supports should be designed and used to avoid damage and stress to fragile materials. These supports should be made of acid-free materials and should be sufficiently strong to provide support for the duration of the exhibit. Book pages should be held open with polyester ribbons. Books should never be forced open or

unnaturally restrained and positioned for display. All supports should be as visually and physically unobtrusive as possible and should be clean, well-crafted, and of uniform materials and appearance.

b) Permanent Physical Changes In the Library Building:
Any requests to change permanently the library building, such as placing nails in the walls, should be made in writing to the Exhibits Committee well ahead of the planned exhibit date. Only in rare cases will such permission be granted.

4. Length of Exhibit

Length of exhibit will vary depending on the nature of the exhibit and the demands of the schedule. Normally, exhibits may run from one week to six weeks. Exceptions may be made with the approval of the Exhibits Committee.

IV. EXHIBITOR RESPONSIBILITY

An Exhibits Committee representative who is assigned to an exhibit is responsible for coordinating the installing and dismantling to an agreed-upon timeframe with the exhibitor. The exhibitor will cover special costs incurred in mounting the exhibit, including the repair of any damage to the building or library property caused in installation or removal of the exhibit. The exhibitor will provide suitable descriptive annotations (as per exhibit procedures) for prior approval.

Exhibits should be mounted within two days of the specific start dates. Failure to do so may result in forfeiture of the time and space allocated for the exhibit date. Materials must be removed promptly at the close of the exhibit period. If the exhibitor cannot meet the schedule agreed upon, the College Librarian should be notified immediately.

V. SPECIAL ARRANGEMENTS AND REQUIREMENTS

A. Security and Insurance

Loaned objects and materials are afforded the same security protection as that of all library materials but it is recommended that the exhibit originator make arrangements to secure insurance coverage for rare or extremely valuable items. Additional security cannot be provided by the Abell Library. If a specific valuation is placed on exhibited items, the dollar amount should be reported to the College Librarian.

B. Physical Arrangement

An exhibit should normally be accessible to everyone, with special provisions made, if possible, to accommodate the handicapped. An exhibit must not constitute a physical hazard or impede research or regular library use.

VI. CONDITIONS AND RESTRICTIONS

The Abell Library requires the exhibitor to comply with the following conditions prior to mounting the exhibit:

A. Submit an application form to the Library Exhibits Committee well ahead of the date planned for mounting the exhibit.

B. Specify the date desired and secure approval for the date and duration of the exhibit. Alert the Committee to secure necessary clearances for any special events scheduled in conjunction with the exhibit which would affect library services or utilize library facilities.

C. At least two (2) weeks prior to the exhibit schedule a meeting with the Exhibits Committee representative for an exhibit preparation review. Included in this review is a diagram and/or description of proposed arrangement materials. Annotations should be bibliographically and grammatically correct. If additional signs are needed plans for them should be submitted at this time.

D. Each exhibitor, unless utilizing library materials, will sign an agreement releasing Austin College from responsibility for loss or damage to non-library materials used in a given exhibit.

EXHIBIT GUIDELINES
FOR
WILSON ART GALLERY

ARTIST RESPONSIBILITIES:

To provide own assistance in transporting, hanging, and taking down show.

To post title of show, name of artist, dates of show and reception on bulletin board located at the entrance of the Gallery. Lettering will be provided for bulletin board.

Artist needs to provide 3x5 index cards with the title for each piece of art work typed upon it. Each card should be placed next to/under art work with clear piece of plexi-glass placed over index card. The Gallery will provide plexi-glass.

If needed, re-direction of lighting and special cases should be arranged with the Gallery assistant.

Wilson Art Gallery Stands for Sculptures.

new pedestals
8- 21" x 37"
2- 31" x 37"

These above pedestals have covers. Their sizes are as follows:

plexi-glass covers
4- 16" x 16" x 34"
3- 18" x 18" x 27"
1- 20" x 20" x 37"
2- 31" x 31" x 36"

old pedestals
2- 10 1/2" x 10 1/2 x 41"
1- 16" x 14 1/2" x 34"
1- 14" x 13 1/2" x 36"
1- 14" x 12 1/2" x 39"
1- 14" x 10 1/2 x 41"
1- 11 1/2" x 10 1/2" x 36"

A price list may be posted if desired.

To provide typed information on show and artist background on a 8x10 sheet of paper to be placed in insert inside of Gallery. This may be the same information used for your publicity.

ASSISTANCE WITH SHOWS:

Artist needs to provide own assistance in bringing in, hanging
up, and taking down show. Artist must provide any special
tools or equipment as Gallery tools are very limited.

Any special hanging displays or lighting need to be arranged
at least one week in advance.

DIMENSIONS:

Artists will be given exact measurements of the Gallery.

DONATIONS:

Artist may donate an art work to the college provided that a
donation form from the library is filled out.

HOURS FOR THE GALLERY:

Gallery hours directly coincide with the LeMoyne College
Library hours.

Artist will be given hours that the Library is open during the
show. For a recorded message of the hours, please call 445-
4153.

INSURANCE:

Each artist must fill out and return an insurance form
provided by the Gallery before starting work on the show.

INVITATIONS:

**ALL INFORMATION MUST BE GIVEN TO COMMUNICATIONS SIX TO EIGHT
WEEKS PRIOR TO OPENING DATE OF THE SHOW.**

Artist needs to provide a slide of exhibit to be used for
invitation.

Invitations are usually done in black and white on in-house
card stock, however; arrangements can be made for them to be
processed in color. Artist may meet with the Publications
Coordinator to discuss the size and other invitation features.
At the time of the meeting, artist must provide the title of
show, dates of the show, and reception date. This meeting
should be at least **eight** weeks in advance of show.

Artist may have a maximum of 200 invitations, however;
the artist is responsible for both the postage and addressing
of the invitations.

PUBLICITY:

Background information of the artist and the show must be
given to Communications at least <u>six</u> weeks prior to opening
date of show.

RECEPTION:

A small reception will be hosted by the Gallery.

Foods provided usually include:

    dessert tray

    vegetable tray
    cheese and crackers
    mint candies
    non-alcoholic punch (alcohol may not be served due to
    college regulations.)

An estimate of the artist's guest is needed to prepare enough
food for the reception.

Artist may supplement additional food if desired.

June 2, 1994

ar/pm

GUIDELINES FOR DISPLAYS

The Gregg-Graniteville Library welcomes the use of the display case by USCA faculty, staff, and recognized campus organizations.

A. The Head of Public Services is responsible for scheduling and approval of all displays.

B. Library displays have first priority.

C. All other display reservations are taken on a first-come, first-served basis.

D. Each display must include the name of the responsible individual or sponsoring organizations and must be clearly visible within the case.

E. Faculty, staff and student displays are expected to serve an educational purpose supportive of the mission of USCA. They may also promote the programs and activities of recognized campus organizations. The display case is not available for the publicizing of partisan political, social, artistic, or other viewpoints. The Library reserves the right to deny use of the display case for these purposes.

F. All materials are locked within the display case. However, the Library is not responsible for the theft or defacement of materials which may occur during the time in which they are displayed.

G. The assembling and disassembling of display materials will be the sole responsibility of the displayer. Displays must be assembled within a twenty-four hour period, preferably during Friday afternoons, Saturdays, or Sundays. This applies likewise to the disassembling of displays.

* * *

I have read the "Guidelines for Displays" and agree to abide by them:

Person (or organizational representative) responsible. Include name of the organization if applicable.

Signature:_____
Address: _____
Telephone: Home:_____ Work:_____
Date Signed:_____

CALIFORNIA STATE UNIVERSITY SAN MARCOS LIBRARY EXHIBITS POLICY

PURPOSE

The purpose of CSU San Marcos Library exhibits is to provide a forum for the free exchange of ideas through the visual arts. Space is provided for both CSUSM student and faculty-generated exhibits as well as for the arts community at large.

CRITERIA & *PHILOSOPHY* FOR EXHIBITION IN THE CSUSM LIBRARY

All exhibits must be approved by the Library's Arts Committee *and the Dean of Library Services* and are subject to the following considerations:

- Exhibits should support and stimulate library users' educational and cultural interests and must reflect and uphold the university's mission statement. *Exhibits which support the curricular goals of the CSUSM Visual & Performing Arts program and other campus academic programs will be given priority. Exhibits which have possible development mplications will be considered secondarily.*

- Since the CSUSM Library is **not** a gallery, the *Library* Arts Committee, exercising curatorial discretion, will determine if a proposed exhibit is appropriate for the library setting *and assumes responsibility for all aesthetic judgements.*

- Once the Arts Committee has met with the artist(s) and determined a particular exhibit to be appropriate in content for the library setting, the Library Arts Committee will determine the extent to which library walls and ceiling structures might be compromised *and will work with Facilities personnel on appropriate arrangements.*

- Facilities personnel will be responsible for restoring the integrity of the space (spackle, paint etc.). Therefore, Facilities has the right to refuse an exhibit if the extent of potential damage is determined to be very high and/or irreparable.

SECURITY

The University and the Library does not take responsibility for the security of exhibit items. Insurance *for each exhibit will* be requested in advance.

*** Permanent pictures and posters hung in the public area of the library are to be framed or core mounted.

5/1/95

Herrick Memorial Library
Display/Exhibit Policy

Herrick Library endorses the articles of the American Library Association's Library Bill of Rights. Those relating to displays and exhibits state that:

Libraries should provide materials and information presenting all points of view on current and historical issues... (Article 2)

Libraries which make exhibit spaces...available to the public they serve (*in this case, the Alfred University community*) should make such facilities available on an equitable basis, regardless of the beliefs or affiliations of individuals or groups requesting their use. (Article 6)

Additionally, it is the policy of the Educational Services Department to present displays which enhance educational messages, induce thought, provoke comment, support campus programs, promote awareness of world-wide events; in short, with an educational mission.

In supporting a broad expression of diverse points of view, the library welcomes suggestions and offers of materials for display which serve the informational, educational, cultural, and recreational needs and interests of the university community, while reserving our prerogative to make final determination on the appropriateness of a display.

We recognize that some patrons may, from time to time, find a display personally objectionable and, while it is not our policy to censor an exhibit which conforms to our guidelines, patrons may post comments in the Suggestion Box and/or ask for a "Display Request/ Comment Form" at the Information Desk and direct their comments to the head of Educational Services, Pam Lakin.

All student organizations sanctioned by the University are encouraged to use the display case set aside for this purpose. The following guidelines will be followed:
1. Displays will be scheduled on a first-come, first-served basis.
2. One Display per year/per organization.
3. Displays may be exhibited for up to one month.
4. Displays must conform to Alfred University policies (for example, on discrimination or substance abuse)
5. Displays will be scheduled by the Educational Services Librarian. Be prepared to describe your proposal as well as what materials will be used, and to schedule times for both installation and removal of displays.
6. The Library will use the designated space if no student organization has requested time.

The library will make every effort to protect material displayed, but cannot assume responsibility for possible damage or theft of any item exhibited. All items placed in the library are done so at the owner's risk.

To request display time and space you may fill out a form available at the Information Desk, or call or e-mail Pam Lakin at 871-2231/2184, or flakin@bigvax.alfred.edu   2/96

OBERLIN COLLEGE LIBRARY -- EXHIBITS POLICY

Exhibit Purpose and Content

The purpose of exhibits in the library is to educate and inform viewers about persons, events, and situations of current or historical interest through the use of library resources.

Exhibits must provide background or other subject enhancement beyond the mere publicizing of an event or display of art objects, and should include material from a variety of sources. Exhibits must include and/or refer to materials in the library's collections.

Proposed exhibits which emphasize library activities and collections take first precedence. Those relating to Oberlin College take second precedence.

Who May Exhibit in Oberlin College Libraries?

- Any member of the Oberlin College Community, in affiliation with an established campus organization (i.e., an academic or administrative department, a chartered student organization, etc.)
- Organizations not affiliated with Oberlin College, but with an Oberlin College sponsor. affiliated with a campus organization as defined above.

Procedure for Obtaining Approval of a Proposed Exhibit

- Obtain an Exhibit Proposal Form from the Exhibits Coordinator.
- Return the completed Form at least two weeks before the exhibit opening date. Exhibits of major proportions, involving large amounts of material, special display equipment and insurance provisions, may require notification six to twelve months in advance of the opening date.
- Receive response from the Exhibits Coordinator:
    1) Approval granted, library liaison designated.
    2) Approval withheld pending clarification of specified details or fulfillment of indicated contingencies.
    3) Approval denied, for reasons indicated by the Exhibits Coordinator.
- Exhibits prepared by librarians in their departments or branches need not be approved, but a form must be filed for informational and scheduling purposes.

Procedures to Mount and Dismount Approved Exhibits

The exhibitor should work with the designated liaison to verify the schedule and resolve any problems involving library equipment and materials. Liaisons will not assist in the actual preparation, mounting or dismounting of exhibits. This is the sole responsibility of the person who submits the Exhibit Proposal Form. Mounting and dismounting of exhibits should be done between 8:30 a.m. and 5 p.m. on weekdays.

An exhibit may be cancelled or removed if it does not conform to this Policy statement and other Attachments.

Library reference service and the expertise of other staff subject specialists is available to exhibitors, as to all other library users, for guidance in the location of relevant library materials, assistance in preparation of exhibit-related bibliographies, and consultation on exhibit technique.

Rev. 11/91

Oberlin College Library
Oberlin, Ohio

OBERLIN COLLEGE LIBRARY -- EXHIBITS POLICY
ATTACHMENT A

GUIDELINES FOR SAFE AND PROPER DISPLAY

General Guidelines

- ALL MATERIALS MUST BE DISPLAYED IN AN ARCHIVALLY CORRECT MANNER --
  i.e. they must suffer no damage nor be altered in any way by being placed
  on exhibit.

- Any material touching the pages of a book or manuscript must be acid free.

- Material not in its original format, i.e. photographs, photocopies, etc.,
  or ephemera can be displayed as the exhibitor wishes.

Books, Scores, and Manuscripts

- Manuscripts should be mounted on or matted in acid free board or paper.
  Self-adhesive tape, thumb tacks and pins should not be used directly on the
  material. They can be used to hold the mat or mounting board on display.

- Books and scores when open should be supported in a cradle. They should be
  held open with strips of Mylar. (The use of paper clips, rubber bands, or
  heavy objects to hold books open is damaging to the book.) If standing,
  they should be held upright and square between bookends. When displayed at
  an angle they should be adequately supported.

Other Library Materials

- Sound recordings: Only album covers or other containers, loose liner notes
  and other printed material associated with a sound recording may be
  exhibited. The disc, tape or cassette itself must never be part of an
  exhibit.

- Other materials: Musical instruments and other artifacts should be
  prepared for display in consultation with the Exhibits Coordinator liaison
  and other specialists as needed.

Descriptive Information

- Display lettering and explanatory information should be neat and accurate.

- Ownership of items on display should be clearly identified.

- The organization or group sponsoring the exhibit must be visibly and
  prominently shown on a disclaimer form provided by the library.

NORTH CENTRAL COLLEGE

OESTERLE LIBRARY

EXHIBITS POLICY

The exhibit cases(s) in Oesterle Library are available to the North Central College community for display under the supervision of the Reference Services Librarian. Faculty, staff, and student groups that are registered with the NCC Office of Student Activities may apply to mount an exhibit in Oesterle Library.

Listed below are some general guidelines for exhibits.

1. Written application to reserve a display case must be made to the Reference Services Librarian at least two months in advance. The subject of the display must be described in the application.

2. The subject of all exhibits must have some connection to North Central College, Oesterle Library, or information resources.

3. Exhibits must follow the North Central College Statement of Responsibilities and all other North Central College policies. It is important to recognize that the library is a public building, and all exhibits therein should not detract from the mission of North Central College.

4. Exhibits must be mounted by the 1st of the month or a date agreed to by the Reference Services Librarian and the exhibitor.

5. Exhibits must remain in the case for at least one month or for a period agreed to by the Reference Services Librarian and the exhibitor.

6. Exhibits must be removed at the end of the agreed upon period, in time for the next exhibit to be put up.

7. The Reference Services Librarian, in consultation with the Director of Library Services, makes all exhibit decisions.

cas/cm
Approved by Library Committee
5/28/96

POSITION DESCRIPTIONS
[Excerpts]

Note: Respondents provided position description excerpts for library staff members who had partial responsibility for displays and exhibits.

POSITION DESCRIPTIONS

Bowdoin College
Brunswick, Maine

TITLE: *Special Collections Assistant*

Tasks, Duties and Responsibilities --

Prepare minor and major exhibits. Design and write exhibition material and place exhibits in cases and other display areas. Produce exhibition notes. Schedule, prepare, mount and return travelling exhibits.

Kalamazoo College
Kalamazoo, Michigan

TITLE: *Reference Librarian*

General Responsibilities --

The library's bibliograohic and information technology program which includes: providing liaison with the faculty and providing library instruction for individual classes; directing the library's Freshman Orientation program; presenting workshops for students, faculty, staff and alumni as needed; preparing guides to the library's collection and services, including those presented on K-Info; contributing to the library newsletter; and creating educational and informational bulletin boards.

Moorhead State University
Moorhead, Minnesota

TITLE: *Circulation/Reference Librarian*

Responsibilities and Authorities --

11. (out of 15) Responsible for coordinating and initiating library newsletter and displays.

D'Youville College
Buffalo, New York

TITLE: *Administrative Secretary, Library*

Responsibilities --

13. (out of 14) Plan and mount library displays on a rotational basis. 2%

POSITION DESCRIPTIONS

Spring Hill College
Mobile, Alabama

TITLE: *Reference Assistant/Paraprofessional*

Description of Duties and Responsibilities --

7. (out of 10) Schedules, plans, and executes library displays.

Southern Arkansas University
Magnolia, Arkansas

TITLE: *Cataloging Library Technical Assistant*

Duty Areas --

Exhibits are prepared and displayed in six cases in the Library. Each case is changed in a timely manner.

California State University, San Marcos
San Marcos, California

TITLE: *Library Assistant I*

My mission is to provide necessary support to the operation of Arts & Lectures in order to ensure timely, accurate and complete publicity, accounts management and clerical service.

TITLE: *Library Assistant I*

My mission as a staff member of Arts & Lectures is to support the curriculum through the many concerts, lectures and art exhibits held at CSUSM. I also participate in community outreach through this involvement.

Berry College
Mount Berry, Georgia

TITLE: **Archivist**

Duties and Responsibilities --

6. (out of 9) Create and maintain appropriate exhibits in the archives display cases.

POSITION DESCRIPTIONS

State University of New York, New Paltz
New Paltz, New York

> TITLE: *Secretary I*
>
> *Job Description* --
>
> 8. (out of 11) Exhibit Program: Coordinates the public exhibition program in the entrance hallway of STL. This usually includes eighteen or more displays per year. Schedules and reviews each display prior to the exhibition to meet lighting, space, back drop and other formal and stylistic requirements. Confirmation letters, contracts, and College ionsurance certificates are prepared and tracked.
>
> CRITERIA FOR EVALUATION: Exhibits reflect the Library's interest in the artistic and educational production of the College community, first, and the surrounding communities in addition. The booking dates, exhibitors, phone numbers and addresses are up to date and clear. Necessary documents are prepared at least 24 hours in advance of the exhibit. Keys to cases are available for placing and striking exhibits.

Otterbein College
Westerville, Ohio

> TITLE: *Reference Librarian*
>
> *Job Description* --
>
> 5. Coordinates creation and mounting of displays on the 1st and 2nd floors of the library.

ANNUAL REPORTS
[departmental and excerpts]

Note: Respondents provided departmental annual reports and excerpts from their library's annual reports.

WILLIAM PATERSON COLLEGE
Sarah Byrd Askew Library

Exhibits Committee

Accomplishments, 1992/93

Campus cooperation, community outreach, art, and poetry - we had them all! Once again, the Exhibits Committee had a productive and exciting year. Among our well-received displays were several that involved the loan of information and materials from sources outside the Library. We were particularly pleased to cooperate with the College Relations Office, the Child Care Center, and the community of Ridgewood.

Exhibits fall into five different areas: major lobby exhibits, current awareness, literary/musical/historical, general interest, and curriculum materials. Each of the exhibit cases had designated subject approaches, and highlights of each are mentioned below:

1. **Major lobby exhibits:**

   Distinguished lecture series. Once again, the main exhibit included photos and information on each speaker. The display was followed up with individual displays on each speaker at the time of the lecture. Feedback from the College Relations Office has been very positive for this support of their efforts.

   Jefferson and Hamilton. The exhibit coincided with the Jefferson Lecture held on April 28, 1993, and included Library materials and the bibliography on the lecture.

   Photography. As part of the Outreach Program, this exhibit included Library books on photography and a sampling of work of members of the Ridgewood Camera Club.

   History of mapmaking. This well received exhibit included maps of all types, books, and globes.

2. **General interest exhibits:**

   Architecture. Designed as an overview of different architectural styles, this display included photographs, cameras, and Library books.

   Art work from the WPC Child Care Center. The work of the children enrolled in the WPC Child Care Center was displayed in this exhibit.

   Australia. This interdisciplinary display included artifacts, books, maps, and pictures.

William Paterson College
Wayne, New Jersey

2. Current awareness:

Exhibits included memorials to noted figures such as Arthur Ashe, Helen Hayes, and Rudolf Nureyev. Displays were also constructed to coordinate with various college activities such as the jazz series and assorted campus workshops. Also included was a special display honoring the Library Student Assistant Awardees.

3. Literary/musical/historical:

Personages such as George Gershwin, Mary Cassatt, Steven Spielburg, and Meryl Streep were featured during their birthday or death months.

4. Curriculum materials:

Curriculum materials and juvenile literature featured such topics as American Indians, field trips, dictionaries, teaching aids, and Maurice Sendak.

Once again, thanks are due to Millie DePow and Kris Owens for all their help and ideas, as well as their willingness to respond quickly when a world shaking event occurs. We will keep exhibits in our hearts and minds, and come back to the new library with a full slate of ideas.

Amy Job   6/14/93

Connecticut College
Charles E. Shain Library

(Excerpts from recent annual reports of the Special Collections Librarian)

Exhibit Titles 1994-1995

"Mississippi in the Sixties: Civil Rights Memorabilia from the Collection of Lonnie Braxton, Class of 1986" (Mounted in conjunction with a College-sponsored symposium on Civil Rights.)

"Lights and Color, Joy and Hope: Children's Books from the Helen O. Gildersleeve Collection, Charles E. Shain Library" (Christmas and Hannukah)

"To Listen With the Heart: Realizing Feminism in the Community" (Student projects combining graphics and text, prepared by the professor and students of a Government seminar)

"Rudolph Ruzicka: Engraver, Designer, Typographer 1883-1978" (Co-curated by an art history professor and the special collections librarian, with many original materials borrowed from the Ruzicka collections at the Boston Athenaeum; included gallery talk and reception.)

"Highlights from the Sheaffer-O'Neill Collection" (Photographs, clippings, letters, and books from the library's large archive on Nobel and Pulitzer prize-winning playwright Eugene O'Neill, who lived in New London as a child and young adult. A similar exhibition was held in November, 1993, and the flier for that occasion is included with the packet.)

Exhibit titles 1995-1996

"Recent Acquisitions in the Department of Special Collections"

"Mothers and Others: Victorian Literary Association Books, Drawings, and Letters from the Collection of Mark Samuels Lasner, Class of 1974" (Publicized on several Internet lists; copy of exhibition catalogue included in packet.)

"The Czech Experience" (Books, graphics and memorabilia collected by faculty during a summer seminar in Prague.)

"Rainy Nights and Snow: 20th Century Japanese Woodblock Prints from the Library Collection"

"William Morris and the Kelmscott Press"   A centenary display of the sixteen Kelmscott Press titles (and two leaves) owned by the Charles E. Shain Library, with related books, a Morris and Co. wall hanging, and autograph letters by May Morris, his daughter. (Publicized on several Internet lists, with plans for illustrated features in the local newspaper, the College newspaper, and the *Connecticut College Magazine;* as this questionnaire is being completed the *C.C. Magazine* has just won the 1996 gold medal for best national college magazine).

D'Youville College
Buffalo, New York

NOTE: From the library annual report.

4. Displays

6/94	Mythology and Folklore - Jill, Sheila
9/94	Hispanic Heritage Month - Grace, Josephine
10/94	Halloween - Courtlann, Cher
11/94	Internet - Ro, Noreen
	Dinosaurs - Courtlann
1/95	Black History Month - Leon, Jill
3/95	Newbery & Caldecott Award Books - Leon, Jill
	Women's History Month - Jill, Sheila
	March is Social Work Month - Grace, Josephine
4/95	Publish or Perish - Leon, Jill
4/95	Nobel Prize-winning Authors-National Library Week - Leon, Jill
5/95	National Nurses Week - Michele, Judy
	Get Fit - Michele, Judy

NOTE: From the Acquisitions Department annual report.

Displays done, as scheduled: Hispanic Heritage Month, Sept.–Oct. 1994, upstairs; March is Social Work Month. Begins with me and ends with us. Stop the violence, March 1995, downstairs. Faculty associated with both expressed their thanks.

New book displays continue to be very effective, as reported last year. However, no progress was made on a better system for displaying new materials. As a result, only a limited number, of highest interest, get displayed.

Wolfgram Memorial Library
Widener University
Chester, Pennsylvania

REQUEST FORMS

OBERLIN COLLEGE LIBRARY -- EXHIBIT PROPOSAL FORM

1.   NAME, ADDRESS AND PHONE NUMBER OF PERSON RESPONSIBLE FOR EXHIBIT:

2.   AFFILIATION: (Within O.C.: dept., group, etc. Not O.C.: affiliation and O.C. sponsor)

3.   NAME, ADDRESS AND PHONE NUMBER OF PERSON RESPONSIBLE FOR MOUNTING EXHIBIT:

     NAME, ADDRESS AND PHONE NUMBER OF PERSON RESPONSIBLE FOR DISMOUNTING EXHIBIT:

4.   NAME OF EXHIBIT:

5.   DATES OF EXHIBIT: STARTING DATE: ENDING DATE:

6.   BRIEF DESCRIPTION OF EXHIBIT: (see Policy and Attachment A. Use extra sheets if needed.)

     a.   Scope of exhibit.

     b.   Occasion being celebrated, if any (i.e. birthday, anniversary, lecture, etc.):

     c.   Other related events occurring on campus or off campus.

     d.   Materials to be exhibited by type and quantity.

7.   LIBRARY MATERIALS TO BE USED AND/OR CITED:

8.   DATE OF FINAL MEETING WITH EXHIBITS COORDINATOR (must be at least one week in advance of exhibit starting date):

9.   EXHIBIT AREA REQUESTED: (see Attachment B)

10. EQUIPMENT REQUESTED: (see Attachment B)

11. SUPPLIES NEEDED, if any:

12. PUBLICITY PLANNED: In Oberlin:

     Out of Oberlin:

(Copies of all press releases, advertising, broadsides and clippings related to the exhibit should be sent to the Exhibits Coordinator, Oberlin College Library.)

   I have read the Oberlin College Library Exhibits Policy Statement and other Attachments, and I agree to conform to them.

_____   _____
     Signature of Exhibitor   Date

Oberlin College Library
Oberlin, Ohio

FOR EXHIBITS COORDINATOR USE ONLY

RECEIVED (Date):

APPROVED: (Date):

APPROVAL CONTINGENT UPON:

DENIED (Date):
      (Due to):

EQUIPMENT RESERVED:
      DATES:

MASTER CALENDAR RECORDED: Date:

EXHIBIT COMMITTEE LIAISON:

DATE AND TIME OF MOUNTING EXHIBIT:

DATE AND TIME OF DISMOUNTING EXHIBIT:

ASSISTANCE REQUIRED:

BRANCH LIBRARIAN'S APPROVAL:

REFERENCE AND CIRCULATION DEPARTMENT INFORMED OF EXHIBIT:

CUSTODIANS NOTIFIED 2 DAYS IN ADVANCE: Date:

MARK O. HATFIELD LIBRARY
WILLAMETTE UNIVERSITY
DISPLAY REQUEST FORM

Today's Date:_____

Title of Display:_____

Date Display Starts:_____ to _____

Please include time needed for set-up and clean-up

Sponsoring Organization/Department:_____

Reserved By:_____ Phone:_____

Please describe the theme or idea of your display:

Please indicate special needs:

You are responsible to provide all materials and clean up your display.

Please return this form to Dayna Collins - Hatfield Library

Library Use Only:

Approved By:_____

Comments:_____

_____

_____

cc: Requestor

University of Puget Sound
Tacoma, Washington

LIBRARY SHOWCASE AGREEMENT

NAME: _____ TELEPHONE NUMBER: _____

DEPT/SPONSORING BODY: _____

THEME OF DISPLAY: _____

START DATE: _____ ENDING DATE: _____

SHOWCASE(S) ASSIGNED: ☐ 1   ☐ 4
                       ☐ 2   ☐ 5
                       ☐ 3   ☐ 6

The above listed Department/Sponsoring Body agrees to:

1.   Exhibit a title card indicating the name of the Department/Sponsoring Body, contact person, and telephone number of the contact person, and the beginning and ending date of the display.

2.   Users are responsible for any damage incurred while setting up/taking down their displays (chipped or broken glass, shelves, or wooden cases.)

3.   There is a maximum of one month for displaying. If display is not removed promptly the Library will remove materials.

DACUS LIBRARY EXHIBITS APPLICATION FORM

Contact Person_____   Phone_____

Organization_____   Address_____

Winthrop Dept._____   _____

Exhibits can be requested for 2 or 4 week periods. (Circle one.)
Dates requested:

Statement of general theme, and title of exhibit:

Description of exhibit contents:

Space and/or cases requested (see Exhibits Committee first for
availability):

Other display materials requested:

We will provide a banner if requested. What should the banner say?
(Eight word maximum.)

Winthrop University
Rock Hill, South Carolina

(OVER)

Dacus Library reserves the right to reject any exhibit applications. Priority will be given to Library issues and events. Other groups will be allowed access if content meets exhibit policy criteria and the schedule permits.

IMPORTANT: PLEASE READ AND SIGN THE FOLLOWING STATEMENT

I understand that neither Dacus Library nor Winthrop University will be held responsible for materials used for exhibit. I also agree to take responsibility to transport, display, maintain, and dismantle all exhibit materials.

Signed_____ Date_____

****
FOR EXHIBITS COMMITTEE USE ONLY

Approve_____   Reject_____

Reason if rejected:

Dates assigned to exhibit:

Completely assembled by_____

Completely dismantled by_____

EXHIBIT REQUEST FORM -- ABELL LIBRARY

Proposed Exhibit Title_____

Dates Preferred (Inclusive): From:_____ To:_____

Alternative Dates: From:_____ To:_____

Please include the following on an attached page:

1) Description of exhibit: (List types of materials, such as books, ephemera, media, or other formats; outline scope of exhibit)

2) Source of Materials

3) Physical Requirements: (space needed, number of display cases, etc.).

4) Supplies needed for exhibit (e.g. book stands, easels, fabric, etc.)

5) Publicity and/or correlative events planned.

Approximate value of exhibits (may not be necessary): $_____

Requestor: _____
                    (name, please print)
Sponsoring Organization _____
                                    (name and telephone)
Faculty Sponsor_____
                          (name and telephone)

I agree to be responsible for installing /dismantling the exhibit and agree to remove it promptly at the end of the exhibit period. I have read the Library's Exhibits Policy and acknowledge by my signature below that I accept the conditions and responsibilities stated therein and will hold Austin College and Abell Library harmless for any condition relative to the exhibit beyond general control.

Signature:_____Date_____

Address:_____Phone_____

Austin College
Sherman, Texas

Exhibit: Approved/Denied:_____
                                                    (date)

Comments:

Committee Recommendations:

Approved Dates of Exhibit:
From:_____   To:_____

Placed on Exhibit Calendar: _____
                                                        (date)
Location of Exhibit: _____

Reviewed for Conditions: _____
                                                        (date)
Submit Publicity Information to Committee by:

                          _____
                                        (date)

Scheduled Meeting with Exhibits Committee Representative to install
exhibits by _____
                        (date)

_____   _____
   Exhibits Representative   (Date)

_____   _____
      College Librarian   (Date)

_____

[1] Adapted from the "Arizona State University Libraries Exhibits Policy" dated 9/17/90

Humboldt State University Library
LIBRARY EXHIBITS APPLICATION

PLEASE FILL OUT AND RETURN TO LIBRARY ADMINISTRATION OFFICE, ROOM 107

Name _____ Date _____

Local Address _____ Phone No. _____

_____

Individual or organizational sponsor _____

    Faculty Member _____ Student _____ Other _____

Title of Exhibit _____

Set-up date and time _____

                                        TWO WEEK LIMIT

Take down date and time _____

Exhibit space requested:

  Large fixed glass case (see attached diagram showing dimensions)_____
    (located near main elevator)

  Horizontal Cases (there are three and they are movable) _____
    (located in the main lobby area)

  Hallway Cases (there are two and they are fixed) _____
    (located in hallway outside of Administration Office, Rm. 108)

  Wall area - left of Circulation Desk _____

    Number of hangers requested _____ (see sample hangers in L107)
      (for wall displays--i.e., photographs--we do not provide frames)

     * * * * * * * * *   **PLEASE NOTE**   * * * * * * * * *

INFORMATION BELOW IS WHAT WILL BE DISPLAYED BY YOUR EXHIBIT. Please sign
below acknowledging that you have read and consent to this.

_____
Signature of exhibitor

Fill in information to be displayed:

Title of Exhibit _____

Organizational Sponsor _____

Please direct questions or comments to:

Name of Exhibitor _____

Local phone and/or address _____

_____

Exhibits in the Library are prepared by and reflect the opinions, interests, and efforts of individual University
persons or organizations or members of the wider community. No official University or Library
endorsement is expressed or implied.

EVALUATION/COMMENT FORMS

AFRICAN AMERICAN WOMEN: YESTERDAY, TODAY, TOMORROW

EXHIBIT EVALUATION

Let us know your opinion of the Black History Month Exhibit by checking Yes, No, Excellent, Good, Fair, Poor to the questions listed below:

_____

1. The African American Women exhibit was attractive and interesting reading.

    a._____Yes   b._____No

2. There were African American women that I had little or no knowledge of their contributions to society.

    a. _____Yes   b. _____No

3. I learned that our library does have a wide variety of books to attract me to read more about the heritage of African American Women.

    a._____Yes   b. _____No

4. The information about African American women was not too overpowering, but clear and to the point.

    a. ____Yes   b._____No.

5. I rated the overall exhibit (display cases and floor) as:

    a. Excellent ____   b. Good _____   c. Fair_____   d. Poor _____

Please turn in at the Circulation Desk. Thank you for your opinion about the display.

California State University
San Marcos, California

100 Portraits: Pioneers, Visionaries and Role Models
11-3 through 11-29-95
comments

Art and Culture of Oaxaca
10-30 through 11-29-95
comments

NOTE: Comments were invited in a notebook with headings at the top of
the notebook pages indicating the title of the exhibit.

Title of Exhibit _____

Organizational Sponsor _____

Please direct questions or comments to:
Name of Exhibitor _____

Local phone and/or address _____

_____

Exhibits in the Library are prepared by and reflect the opinions, interests, and efforts of individual University persons or organizations or members of the wider community. No official University or Library endorsement is expressed or implied.

CHALLENGED LIBRARY MATERIALS
AND
DISCLAIMER FORMS

I, _____ (name), understand that
the library cannot be held responsible for the items placed in
the display case and/or on the display screens.

I will remove the items by _____.
If the items are not removed by this date, the library should:
   ___ dispose of them
   ___ other. Please explain.

I can be contacted at: phone number

                address_____
                       _____
                       _____

Signature _____

Date   _____

Grant and Frankford Avenues • Philadelphia. PA 19114 • 215-637-5828

Oberlin College Library
Oberlin, Ohio

DISCLAIMER STATEMENTS

Some libraries included disclaimer statements in their policy statements (see policy statement of Alfred University) or to their evaluation form (see postcard evaluation form of Humboldt State University).

Oberlin College provided this information:

We ran into a somewhat similar problem last year with a one sided exhibition... We decided that the exhibition could stay up but a disclaimer in large type was added indicating that the exhibit was the responsibility of the group which created it (NAME IN LARGE LETTERS) and not of the library. We also added that in the future all exhibits would have to boldly state the same disclaimer. ... This policy is aimed primarily at student and outside exhibits, not at those created in the library.

Oberlin College Library
Oberlin College
Oberlin, Ohio

CHALLENGED LIBRARY MATERIALS FORM

TITLE:_____

AUTHOR:_____

   [ ] Book   [ ] Periodical   [ ] Video   [ ] Other

PUBLISHER:_____

INITIATED BY: _____

ADDRESS: _____

CITY: _____STATE_____ZIP CODE_____

TELEPHONE: _____

DO YOUR REPRESENT: [ ] Self   [ ] Organization   [ ] Other

IF ORGANIZATION, LIST NAME, AND ADDRESS BELOW:

_____

_____

1. To what extent do you object to the work or items cited above? Be specific and cite page
   (s), photograph, et cetera. _____
   _____
   _____
   _____
   Use separate sheet if necessary.

2. What do you believe is the theme of the work? _____
   _____

3. Are you aware of the professional and literacy critic reviews?
      [ ] Yes   [ ] No

4. As an academic information center library supporting all points of view, what do you

Fort Valley State College
Fort Valley, Georgia

suggest to be done with challenged material (s)?

____Keep in a caged or supervised area

____Reclassify

____Other. Explain _____

_____

_____

Signature_____

Date _____

Mikkelsen Library
Augustana College
Sioux Falls, South Dakota

INSURANCE FORMS

WILSON ART GALLERY
INSURANCE FORM FOR ART EXHIBITS

LOCATION: Le Moyne College Library, First floor

DATES OF EXHIBIT: From (___/___/___) to (___/ ___/ ___)
                       mo., day, yr.   mo., day, yr.

NAME OF ARTIST (OR GROUP):_____

TITLE/DESCRIPTION OF WORKS	ESTIMATED VALUE (OR PRICE)

DATE RECEIVED:_____

SIGNATURE OF ARTIST(S):_____

California State University
San Marcos, California

Memorandum

DATE: January 31, 1996

TO: Deborah Smith, Executive Vice President's Office

FROM: Dannis Mitchell, Arts & Lectures

RE: "A Journey Through the Process" art exhibit in Library and 5th floor of Craven Hall from 1-31-96 through 3-3-96]

CC: Bonnie Biggs

Please insure the above exhibit for a total of $25,350.00. Attached is a list of the 26 paintings to be insured.

JUGBELLY STUDIO

Insurance Form

"A JOURNEY THROUGH THE PROCESS"
Dorothy Annette

All Paintings are Oil on Canvas

1.	Little Red Dress II	$1,250
2.	Frying Pans & Skillets	$700
3.	Chair w/ apple (Charcoal)	$250
4.	Book w/ apple (Charcoal)	$250
5.	Little Red Teapot (private collection)	$1,225
6.	Goddess In Training: The Crown.	$350
7.	Diversity	$695
8.	Dying: Flower Bouquet	$800
9.	Study for Japanese Teapot	$275
10.	Stalwart Teapot (private collection)	$1,250
11.	Renaissance Red Teapot	$275
12.	Noble Teapot & Cup (Yellow Teapot w/cup)	$355
13.	Loner Teapot (private collection)	$1,250
14.	Tools of the Trade	$800
15.	My Bucket Runneth Over (private collection)	$2,250
16.	Sexy Little Teapot (private collection)	$2,250
17.	The Phoenix (private collection)	$2,250
18.	Japanese Teapot	$1,450
19.	Queen Bee Teapot	$1,300
20	Long Time Friend	$275
21	Survivor	$700
22	B.B. La Femme	$700
23.	Milk Bucket	$900
25.	Old Office Chair (private collection)	$2,250
26.	Mom (private collection)	$1,250
Total		**$25,350**

LOAN AGREEMENT FORMS

This Agreement is made between [Full name and address of Lender] ("Lender") and The University of the South ("University");

RECITALS

Lender is the owner of the _____ ("Work") described in this Agreement; and

The parties desire that University have custody and possession of the Work in its facilities located at the Jesse Ball duPont Library for the purposes of public display and enjoyment, conservation, and scholarship befitting its unique character; and

The parties desire by this Agreement to provide for the parties' respective interests in the Work and for procedures and understandings governing its use, custody, protection and public enjoyment.

TERMS

In consideration of the mutual covenants and conditions set forth in this Agreement, and for good and valuable consideration, the parties agree as follows:

Description of Work.

The work which is the subject of this Agreement is a [describe work].

Duration of Loan.

This Loan shall be for a term of ____ months/years, beginning on [date], which is when University shall physically take possession of Work, and ending on the loan termination date of [date], which is when University shall relinquish physical possession of Work to Lender.

This Loan is renewable and the duration of any such renewal shall be determined by written mutual consent of the parties.

Consideration.

As consideration for receiving the loan of Work, University agrees to perform the obligations set forth in this Agreement.

Receipt and Return of Work.

Lender shall deliver Work, freight prepaid, to University at the following address: _____ . **OR**
University or its agent shall take possession of Work on the Loan Commencement Date directly from Lender.

University shall deliver Work, freight prepaid, to Lender within thirty (30) days of the termination of this Agreement. **OR**

Lender or its agent shall take possession of Work on the termination date of this Agreement directly from University.

<u>Condition, Use, and Care of Work.</u>

Lender certifies that Work is in good condition unless and except as specifically noted: _____.

University agrees that Work will be used solely for non-commercial display at the site[s] noted in this Agreement, which shall not preclude the levying upon University patrons of fees to visit University. University may, in its discretion, display and use Work as a part of a regular, special, or theme exhibition upon its premises.

University agrees to comply with its normal rules and procedures, as well as all applicable laws, ordinances, and regulations relating to possession, use, and maintenance of work. University at its own cost and expense shall take all reasonable action necessary to avoid damage, destruction, abuse, misuse, or deterioration of Work.

University shall not loan Work for exhibition or other usage away from the premises of University without the written consent of Lender.

Upon termination of this Agreement, University shall return Work to Lender in as good condition as when University took possession thereof, ordinary wear, tear, degradation and inherent vice excepted.

<u>Loss, Damage and Indirect or Unallocated Expenses.</u>

University shall be liable to Lender for the full amount of uninsured loss of or damage to Work and for the full amount of any other loss, damage or expense caused solely by University's negligence. University shall not be responsible for the protection and safekeeping of Work beyond the exercise of such precautions as are taken for the protection and safekeeping of comparable property of its own. University assumes no responsibility in case of loss or damage to Work by reason of uninsurable risks such as inherent vice, war, invasion, hostilities, rebellion, insurrection, riot, civil commotion, nuclear damage, or flood.

<u>Termination of the Loan Agreement.</u>

This Agreement may be terminated by either party by giving the other party ____ days written notice;

Reproduction and Examination.

Except as otherwise specified in this Agreement, or without the written consent of Lender, University agrees not to sketch, photograph, reproduce, or otherwise reproduce Work for commercial purposes, and agrees to undertake reasonable measures not to allow others to reproduce Work for commercial purposes, without express written consent of Lender.

Conservation.

Except in the case of an emergency to preserve Work, University shall not touch up, reframe, repair or restore Work, nor clean, repair, or remove Work from its frame, or otherwise change, alter, or disturb its physical condition of Work without the written consent of Lender.

Warranty of Title.

Lender warrants that it is the owner of Work, that in its best belief Work is not presently subject to claims of ownership, lien or encumbrance or to common law or statutory copyright claims of any other person, institution, or domestic or foreign government, and that Lender has complied with all applicable domestic and foreign customs and export/import regulations.

No Personal Liability.

No director, trustee, officer, agent, or employee of either party shall be charged personally with any liability under any term or provision of this Agreement.

Governing Law; Forum.

This Agreement shall be governed by and construed under the laws of the State of Tennessee, which shall also be the forum for any lawsuit between the parties arising from or incident to this Agreement.

Severability.

If any term or provision of this lease is declared by a court of competent jurisdiction to be illegal, void, or unenforceable, that shall not affect the validity and enforceability of the remaining portions of this Agreement.

Non-Waiver.

The failure of either party to exercise any of its rights under this Agreement for a breach thereof shall not be deemed to be a waiver of such rights, nor shall the same be deemed to be a waiver of any subsequent breach, either of the same provision or otherwise.

Notice.

Any notice to either party hereunder must be in writing, and signed by the party giving it, and either served by hand, by mail through the U.S. Postal Service postage prepaid, registered or certified, return receipt requested, or by an overnight, or other expedited mail or package service, with a receipt showing the delivery has been made, addressed as follows:

To University:

To Lender:

or to such other addressee as may be hereafter designated by written notice.

Headings.

The paragraph headings herein are used only for ease of reference, and do not limit, modify, construe, or interpret any provision of this Agreement.

Assignment.

This Agreement may not be assigned by either party without the express written consent of the other, in advance; the assignee thereof shall have all the rights and remedies of the original parties insofar as the same are assignable. Assignments shall be only as a whole and not as a part, nor as to any part interest therein.

Entire Agreement.

This Agreement (and its attachments, if any) constitutes the entire understanding between the parties with respect to the subject matter hereof and may be amended at any time only upon mutual written agreement of the parties.

IN WITNESS WHEREOF, the authorized representatives of the parties have executed this Agreement on this ____ day of _____, 19__.

The University of the South: Lender:

by _____   by_____
(Signature)   (Signature)

_____   _____
(Printed Name)   (Printed Name)

_____   _____
(Title)   (Title)

OBERLIN

OBERLIN COLLEGE LIBRARY • OBERLIN, OHIO 44074-1532 • Fax: 216/775-8739

Main Library	Art Library	Science Library	Conservatory Library
Mudd Center	Allen Art Building	Kettering Hall	Conservatory of Music
216/775-8285	216/775-8635	216/775-8310	216/775-8280

SPECIAL COLLECTIONS DEPARTMENT

LOAN AGREEMENT FORM

EXHIBITION: Title_____

Location_____

Dates_____

BORROWER: Contact person_____

Institution_____

Address_____

_____

_____

Telephone_____

Fax_____

E-mail_____

LENDER CREDIT LINE: OBERLIN COLLEGE LIBRARY, SPECIAL COLLECTIONS

BOOKS OR OTHER MATERIALS LOANED:

INSURANCE VALUE:

Photography conditions:

Mode of Transportation:

Date materials sent:

Return date:

Rev. 3/96

Oberlin College
Oberlin, Ohio

Conditions governing loans:

1. The borrower will exercise the same care in respect to the loans as it does in the safekeeping of its own property.

2. The loaned material shall remain in the same condition in which it is received. It shall not be mended, cleaned, restored, or rehoused in any way.

3. The borrower will not photocopy or otherwise reproduce the material in whole or in part except with the express written permission of the Special Collections Department of the Oberlin College Library. It is the borrower's responsibility to secure copyright permission for reproduction.

4. Damages, whether in transit or on the premises of the borrowing institution, shall be reported to Oberlin immediately, and all packing materials saved for inspection.

5. The borrowing institution must provide a written description of the exhibition area and cases to be used, and details of security arrangements.

6. The loaned material must be displayed under secure conditions, protected from UV radiation, in low light and within a temperature/humidity range of 65¤ to 75¤F. and 35 to 50% RH, with minimum fluctuations. Adequate and non damaging supports must be used for all materials.

7. No single page or item shall remain on view for longer than three months.

8. The borrower is responsible for including the credit line specified on the items in the exhibition and in any exhibition related published material. One copy each of such published material should be returned with the items to the Oberlin College Library.

9. The borrower is responsible for insurance covering the item(s) from the time it is shipped to the borrowing institution until it is returned to the Oberlin College library. Insurance must be at a level stipulated by Oberlin and will be based on the approximate fair market value of the item.

10. Oberlin College will pay shipping costs to the exhibition but the borrower must pay shipping costs for the return of the items, which must be sent by common carrier as listed overleaf.

I have read the above Loan Agreement and agree to its conditions.

Signed:_____Date:_____

Title_____

Approved for Oberlin College Library Special Collections

Signed:_____Date:_____

Title:_____

Please sign and return both copies to Special Collections, Oberlin College Library, Oberlin, OH 44074. One copy will be returned with the item(s).

Rev. 3/96

AGREEMENT BETWEEN THE SOJOURNER TRUTH LIBRARY AND EXHIBITORS

1. I, _____, representing _____
    _____, certify that I have deposited in the Sojourner
    Truth Library, College at New Paltz, State University of New York, New
    Paltz, New York (Brief description of material exhibited).
    _____
    _____
    My estimate of its value is $_____.

2. This item is on exhibit in the Sojourner Truth Library from
    _____ to _____. That period of exhibit may be
    extended upon the mutual agreement of the exhibitor and the Director of
    the Library. All displays are to be installed and disassembled between
    the hours of 8:45 am and 4:00 pm weekdays only.

3. This item is to be housed and displayed in the Sojourner Truth Library
    in those places designated by the Director of the Library. I agree that
    no part of my exhibit will be installed outside of the locked cabinets
    provided for them.

4. I agree that the Director of the Library may remove the item from its
    location and from public view at any time it is necessary in his
    judgment to do so.

5. I agree that the Sojourner Truth Library, its officers and its employees
    are not responsible in any manner for any loss or damage to this item
    while it is housed in the Library.

6. I agree to take full responsibility for delivering, installing and
    erecting the item in the space designated and for disassembling and
    removing it when its exhibit period is terminated.

7. I agree that all financial costs arising from item six (6) will be borne
    by me.

                              Signed   _____

                             Address   _____

                           Telephone   _____

                                Date   _____

PLANNING FORMS

Art Exhibit Checklist

To be taken care of as soon as an artist and dates of exhibit are confirmed:

___1) Define and reserve wall or floor space needed for exhibit.

___2) Independent Contractor Requisition Form and 204 Vendor Data Record if an honorarium is involved. (Obtain social security number from artist as well as a mailing address.

___3) Begin to request press release information.

___4) Try to get a photo or graphic from the artist for the flyer.

___5) Begin to obtain information to be used in handout.

___6) Notify professors or department if exhibit is course related.

To be taken care of at least three weeks before opening of exhibit:

___1) Send press release information to the Office of Public Affairs.

___2) Make and mail (bulk) flyer or invitation regarding opening (needs 10 mailing days).

___3) Reserve any equipment necessary (including tables for reception).

___4) Send information for Calendar section to the Public Affairs Office.

___5) Arrange for any help necessary from Alan Miles. CC Susan Baksh on any correspondence regarding this.

___6) Arrange for Media Services to photograph exhibit and opening.

To be taken care of one week before opening of exhibit.

___1) Send a copy of flyer or invitation to all faculty and staff. Send 6 copies to Darla Mitchell-Lusky to post around campus.

___2) Make sure that Public Affairs sends out public e-mail regarding exhibit opening.

___3) Send insurance information to Institutional Resources. Address a memo to Pat Farris and send to Deborah Smith (secretary) along with an itemized list of art to be exhibited and its worth.

___4) Create handouts.

___5) Decide what "goodies" will be brought to reception and by who. Make sure the tablecloths are clean.

___6) Check supply of reception "staples" (napkins, stirrers, sugar, creamer, coffee, hot cups, cold cups etc.).

To be taken care a few days before opening of exhibit:

___1) Send an e-mail to all library employees regarding opening of reception.

___2) Make sure that Bonnie has sent out her personal e-mail to "hot list."

___3) Make sure that handouts and any signage necessary are ready.

To be taken care of the day before the reception:

___1) Attach signs to plasticades and place around campus (one in front of the Dome and one outside the library. Attach a "Tomorrow" flag to the sign.

To be taken care of the day of the reception:

-----1) Change "tomorrow" flag to "today" on signs on plasticades and easels.

___2) Put out handouts.

___3) Start coffee aprox. one hour before reception then set up for the rest of the reception.

FOR EXHIBITS COORDINATOR USE ONLY

RECEIVED (Date):

APPROVED: (Date):

APPROVAL CONTINGENT UPON:

DENIED (Date):
      (Due to):

EQUIPMENT RESERVED:
          DATES:

MASTER CALENDAR RECORDED: Date:

EXHIBIT COMMITTEE LIAISON:

DATE AND TIME OF MOUNTING EXHIBIT:

DATE AND TIME OF DISMOUNTING EXHIBIT:

ASSISTANCE REQUIRED:

BRANCH LIBRARIAN'S APPROVAL:

REFERENCE AND CIRCULATION DEPARTMENT INFORMED OF EXHIBIT:

CUSTODIANS NOTIFIED 2 DAYS IN ADVANCE: Date:

CALENDARS AND SCHEDULES

[excerpts]

NYSELIUS LIBRARY EXHIBITS
July 1994-June 1995

July/August: 25th Anniversary of the First Lunar Landing

An exhibit from the collection of Dr. Sharlene McEvoy, associate
professor, of medallions, rocket and spacecraft models. The
display included books written by and about the astronauts and
Apollo mission history as reported in magazines and newspapers.

September: History of Bridgeport Engineering Institute

A display of historical materials from the archive of Bridgeport
Engineering Institute. Photos, newspapers reports and catalogs
were displayed to tract the history of BEI from its founding to the
merger with Fairfield University.

October: Letters Home: Life after Graduation

An exhibit of post graduate mission opportunities available to
graduating Fairfield Students. The display utilized materials from
the collection of Fr. Joseph Schadd, Campus Ministry.

November: Judaic Studies Program

Information about the new Judaic Studies Program and a display of
realia from the collections of Dr. Ellen Umansky, Judaic Studies
Chair, Rabbi James Prosnit, Congregation B'Nai Israel, Fairfield,
Dr. Philip Eliasoph and Mr. Samuel Liskov.

December 1994 - January 1995: Fairfield Archaeology, Ogden House

Mounted with the cooperation of the Fairfield Historical Society,
a display of artifacts discovered by an archaeological dig from
Fairfield's historic Ogden House supervised by Shirley Paustian,
Archaeologist and a member of the Nyselius Library staff.

February 1995: AHANA Handbook/ Multicultural Relations Resource
Center

A display of the newly published AHANA student handbook, resources
available at the Multicultural Resource Center. Exhibit prepared
with the cooperation of the Office of Multicultural Relations.

March 1995: Women's History Month

A display of the resources and programs available through the
campus Women's Resource Center

April 1995: Student Silkscreen Art

A display of student silkscreen art produced during the spring 95
semester and information on the galleries located in Loyola Hall.

Washburn University
Topeka, Kansas

<u>1994-1995</u>   <u>1993-1994</u>

18   7

DISPLAYS

        #Hispanic American--May
        D-Day 50th Anniversary--May/June
        *Tornado Anniversary--June
        Apollo 11 25th Anniversary--July
        *Washburn History--August
        #E.P. Sanders (King lecture)--September
        Native Americans (ILL Development Grant)--September/October
        Banned Books Week--October
        *Carnegie 90th Anniversary--October
        #Alchohol Awareness Week--October
        #*Physical Education History (KHPERD Conference)--October
        *Veterans Day--November
        Staff in Print--December/January
        Martin Luther King Day--January
        *Founders Day (February 6, 1985)--February
        #*Black History Month--February
              (1 case Blacks at Washburn)
        *Women's History Month--March
              (1 case Women at Washburn)
        Earth Day--April

        #Campus department or organization request
        *Archival materials used

BOATWRIGHT LIBRARY EXHIBITS
DISPLAY CASES
1995-1996

MONTH	TOPIC	PERSON(S) RESPONSIBLE
May	Pulitzer Prize Winners	L. McCulley
June	Children's Literature	L. Christner
July	Governor's School	L. McCulley
August	Summer Reading	L. McCulley
September	Food and Drink Cultural Events in Richmond	L. McCulley L. Christner
October	Int. Film Series	MRC
November	Government Documents	B. Sudduth
December	Rare Books/Special Coll.	J. Gwin
January	Faculty Research	M. Whitehead
February	Black History	
March	Women's History	L. McCulley
April	Library Week Modlin Book Award	L. McCulley

CONNECTICUT COLLEGE

Cultural and Sporting Events Open to the Public

Sophia Smith Collection Exhibits, 1994-95

Neilson Library

"Susan B. Anthony at 175: Still Radical After All These Years,"
February 15-June 30, 1995,
Collacott Room
Mounted by Amy Hague and Margaret Jessup in honor of Mary Maples Dunn.

**"Constance Baker Motley and Vivion Lenon Brewer: The Legacy of
Brown v. Board of Education", September 1, 1994-
January 13, 1995**
New books exhibit area
Mounted by Amy Hague in honor of the fortieth anniversary of the Brown decision.

"Special Collections: Selected Gifts and Purchases of the Year,"
featuring Birkby and Garrison gifts
Neilson Front Hall, April-May 1995
SSC selections and captions by Amy Hague and Margaret Jessup.

Reading Room

**"Before and After: Processing Manuscript Collections in the Sophia Smith
Collection", September 1994.**
Mounted by Margaret Jessup for orientation.

"The League of Women Voters of Northampton Seventy-Fifth Anniversary,"
March-April 1995
Mounted by Margery Sly.

Smith College
Northampton, Massachusetts

Smith College Archives Exhibits, 1994-95

Alumnae Gymnasium Reading Room

Picture Mary Maples Dunn
Reading Room, February-August 1995
Mounted by Margery Sly

"In Investigation and In Education":
The Lyman Plant House, 1895-1995
Reading Room, February-August 1995
Mounted by Margery Sly

Neilson Library

Special Collections: Selected Gifts and Purchases of the Year
Neilson front hall, April-May 1995
Mounted by Margery Sly and Barbara Blumenthal

Seelye Hall

Seelye Hall
Seelye Hall, November 1994-January 1995
Mounted by Margery Sly

Lyman Plant House

Smith College Medal Winners: Cornelia Hahn
Oberlander '44 and Lynden Breed Miller '60
Lyman Plant House, February 1995
Mounted by Margery Sly and Susan McGlew

Art Museum

AMS 340b "Biography and Autobiography"
Art Museum, May 1995
Mounted by members of the class

TENTATIVE EXHIBITS CALENDAR[1]
1995/96

MONTH	EXHIBIT	SPONSOR
JUNE	Computerization in the library	EXHIBIT COMMITTEE
JULY	Sixties Radicals and Vietnam	ARCHIVES
JULY 24- AUGUST 8	Graduate Art Student Display-Tracy Price	EXHIBIT COMMITTEE
AUGUST	Women's Suffrage --75 year Anniversary	ARCHIVES
SEPTEMBER	World War II Commemoration	ARCHIVES
OCTOBER	The Anderson Car	ARCHIVES
NOVEMBER	Tillman Hall (100 years of history)	
DECEMBER	Books Written by Winthrop Personnel (Reception for the opening of exhibit)	EXHIBIT COMMITTEE
DECEMBER	Christmas at Winthrop (100 Years of Tradition)	ARCHIVES
JANUARY	Elvis in the Carolinas	ARCHIVES
FEBRUARY	Black History Month	EXHIBIT COMMITTEE
MARCH	Woman's History Month	EXHIBIT COMMITTEE
APRIL	Ten Most Notable S. C. Government Publications of the year	SUSAN SILVERMAN
APRIL	National Library Week	EXHIBIT COMMITTEE
MAY	Distinguished Junior/Distinguished Professor of the Year	EXHIBIT COMMITTEE
JUNE		

July 28, 1995
1. Dates may vary during the year.

BROCHURES AND FLYERS

[excerpts]

MARK SERMAN

THE ROOFS OF ST.PETERSBURG

photographs 1976 -1992

...dedicated to people and places from the past...

underwritten by a generous gift from
mrs.nika thayer of the *vera townsend foundation*
sponsored by *the charles e.shain library* and
the *department of russian studies*

April 2 through April 18, 1993 at the
Charles E.Shain Library
Connecticut College, New London
Connecticut
every day from 9 a.m. till 9 p.m
opening on April 2, 1993
from 4.30 p.m till 6.30 p.m.

telephones: show days - 203-447-1911
other times - 718-830-9215

© m.serman

Bethune-Cookman College
Daytona Beach, California

BEFORE YOU CAN SAY JACKIE ROBINSON:

Black Baseball in America in the Era of the Color Line, 1885-1950

an exhibit which traces in photos and in text the history of Black professional baseball from its inception in the midyears of the 1880s as the color line of race and caste began to appear in explicit form through-out American society, through the 1940s In that decade of terrible warfare, forces were at work which eventually eliminated segregation in professional baseball.

Exhibit on loan to Bethune-Cookman College through Dr. Lawrence Hogan, Professor of History, Union County College, New Jersey, frm March 11 through April 15, 1996. There is no admission charge. Exhibit hours: M-F, 10 AM to 5 PM and Saturday, noon to 5 PM.

Funding for the exhibit was made possible, in part, by the Bethune-Cookman College Student Government Association and Daytona Beach Community College. Contact the B-CC Public Relations office at 90 255-1401, extention 435, for further information.

BREAKING BASEBALL'S COLOR LINE: Jackie Robinson and Fifty Years of Integration 1946-1996

an educational exhibit and conference hosted by BETHUNE-COOKMAN COLLEGE to commemorate Jackie Robinson and the Fiftieth Anniversary of the Integration of Professional Baseball

SCHEDULE OF EVENTS

Monday, March 11 - 10:30 AM.
Carl Swisher Library
Bethune-Cookman College
Exhibit Opening for Volusia County School Children

Friday, March 15 - 3:00-6:00 PM
Conference registration, Treasure Island Inn, Daytona Beach Shores. Sessions 1 & 2, Windward and Leeward rooms. Bus leaves for B-CC at 6:45 PM from in front of the Inn, and returns at 10:00 PM.

Friday, March 15 - 7:00 - 7:45 PM
Exhibit Viewing for Conference attendees, Carl S. Swisher Library Lecturer: James A. Riley, Author

Friday, March 15 - 8:00 - 10:00 PM
Reception and Keynote Speaker, President's Dining Room, Bethune-Cookman College. Speaker: Jules Tygiel, San Francisco State University on "Baseball's Great Experiment Revisited: The Evolving Legacy of Jackie Robinson"

Folk Culture Of Northern Thailand
Performance, Temple Festival, and Regional Identity

•Artifacts •Illustrations •Maps
•Musical Transcriptions

Curated by
**Joe Gray, Sean Hantak, Matt Harder, Robin Harms,
Pamela Moro, Catie Rubba, Dima Strakovsky**

November 27 through December 15

Sheean Library

Illinois Wesleyan University

BALLING SPECIAL COLLECTIONS ROOM
CANISIUS COLLEGE LIBRARY

Welcome to the **Balling Special Collections Room** of the Canisius College Library. The Room was opened in 1988 and is a gift of Balling Construction, Inc. and its employees. The Room actually consists of two separate parts: an inner work and storage room, and an outer reading and display area. The collection remains shelved in the inner room, where control of the materials can be more easily monitored and where the lights can be kept off as much as possible to prevent further deterioration. The outer reading room holds rotating displays of selected portions of the collection and tables for those who need to consult the materials.

The Room is open to the public during hours that are posted. It is available at other times by appointment; please see one of the Reference Librarians if you wish to consult or view any of the materials.

The Balling Special Collections Room houses the most unique and valuable materials in the Library. Included in the collection are medieval manuscripts (such as Books of Hours), early Bibles (published from 1483 on), books relating to the history of the Jesuits, the Charles A. Brady collection (Dr. Brady is an author and former professor at Canisius College), books and maps of early Buffalo, books and journals of the history of Canisius College, books on Irish literature, books autographed by their

BRING A GROUP TO THE CROSBY EXHIBIT

Gonzaga University welcomes groups who would like a special introduction to the Crosby Collection and a tour of his boyhood home. Call the Director of Marketing at (509) 328-4220, Ext. 6371, to make advance arrangements.

WANT TO KNOW MORE ABOUT BING?

Gonzaga's Special Collections Department will be pleased to provide information about Bing's association with Gonzaga University, our growing collection and exhibits, and other information of interest. You may write or call (509) 328-4220, Ext. 3847 between 8 a.m. - 5 p.m. weekdays.

COLLECTION VIEWING HOURS

The Crosbyana Room of the Crosby Student Center is open from 7:30 a.m. to midnight Monday - Friday and from 11 a.m. to midnight on Saturday and Sunday, September through May; 8:30 a.m. to 4:30 p.m. weekdays, and closed holidays, June through August.

ABOUT GONZAGA UNIVERSITY

Gonzaga University is an independent, liberal arts university with a student enrollment around 5,000. One of 28 Jesuit colleges in the United States, Gonzaga also offers accredited degree programs in business administration, engineering and education, as well as degrees in 23 master programs and one doctoral program. The Gonzaga University School of Law is one of three in the state of Washington.

NEWSLETTERS

[excerpts]

THE NEWSLETTER
State University of New York at New Paltz

Spring 1996
Issue No. 2

SOJOURNER TRUTH LIBRARY

THE LIBRARY DISPLAYS

March 1 - 29
WOMEN/VIOLENCE:
TESTIMONY & EMPATHY
Sponsored by Women's Studio
Workshop &
the Women's Studies Department

April 1 - 19
DOCUMENTARY
PHOTOGRAPHS
Sponsored by Professor Francois
Deschamps
Art Studio Department
& his students

April 22 - 30
CARIBBEAN CULTURE
Sponsored by the
Caribbean Student Association

May 1 - 10
MUSLIM CULTURE
Sponsored by the
Muslim Student Organization

May 13 - 24
WORKS IN METAL
Sponsored by
Graduate Students
of the Art Studio Department

July 1 - 31
BARBARA RUSSELL:
WATERCOLORS
Sponsored by the artist

August 12 - September 27
ROCKS AND GEMS
Sponsored by the
Mid-Hudson Valley Gem Society

Connecticut College
New London, Connecticut

The Friends of the Connecticut College Library

Connecticut College
New London, Connecticut

A New Year's Newsletter   January, 1996

Membership in the Friends, New or Renewed

We invite you once again to renew your association with the Connecticut College Library. Your continued interest and support is very important to us. A dues card and envelope are enclosed for your convenience.

We would also be grateful for the names of others who might wish to be associated with this unique cultural institution. Please call Special Collections Librarian Brian Rogers (439-2654) if you have names to suggest. We also welcome your ideas for the occasional programs we sponsor.

A contribution of $50 or more entitles a member to twelve months of borrowing privileges along with the satisfaction of helping to underwrite purchases for Special Collections. We use your contributions to build upon existing strengths in literature, science, history and the arts, with special attention to the arts of the book and children's literature. Some recent acquisitions are described elsewhere in this issue. On occasion a book for the circulating collection is acquired. All such acquisitions receive a bookplate stating that they are the *Gift of the Friends of the Library.*

"Mothers and Others": November Exhibition and Lecture Successful

The exhibition of inscribed Victorian-era books and drawings was well received. A handsome catalogue written by Mark Samuels Lasner and printed at The Stinehour Press, Lunenberg, Vermont, was distributed at the November 9 lecture in the Palmer Room. Mark's authoritative annotations provide a glimpse into the world of Victorian literary life, and are interesting even if one has not seen the exhibition they describe. *Please call or write Brian Rogers if you would like to have a copy.* There is no charge.

An interesting marriage of electronic technology and Victoriana occurred when we offered copies of the catalogue to Victorian literature and art enthusiasts on the Internet. After announcing its availability to the electronic discussion groups for rare books ("EXLIBRIS"), book history ("SHARP-L", the group sponsored by the Society for the History of Authorship, Reading, and Publishing), and groups interested in Victorian Studies and book collecting, we have received 187 requests to date! They have come from North America, Britain, Europe, Australia, and – just last week – Hong Kong!

The Eighteen Lohans

On display in the Palmer Room for an extended period is an unusual set of 18th century Buddhist figurines known as lohans. According to the *Dictionary of Comparative Religion*, lohans have attained Buddhist enlightenment and perfection, and serve as the guardians of Buddhism throughout the world. Each figure is about seven inches tall, and stands on a carved wooden base. The collection is owned by the Department of Chinese.

A public lecture about the lohans, sponsored by the Chinese Department, will be given on *Thursday, Feb. 15,* by Prof. Richard Kent of Franklin & Marshall College, at 4:00 p.m. in Room 210 of Blaustein Humanities Center. His title is *The Chinese Cult of Lohans: Depictions of Guardians of the Buddhist Law.*

INSIDE WILLAMETTE

Weekly

....

ROSES ARE RED, VIOLETS ARE BLUE; HERE'S SOME POETRY NEWS FOR YOU

Did you know that the month of April is set aside to celebrate the art of poetry? Well, it is, and during National Poetry Month, the Hatfield Library is sponsoring a multifaceted exhibit featuring selected volumes of poetry displayed in a unique and imaginative manner, along with poems written by students from Robert Hackett's Imaginative Writing class. In addition, a visual display incorporating images and poetry from the work of Yeats and Seamus Heany has been assembled by students from Carol Long's Irish Laureate class. It's all located on the second floor of the library, so, hurry on down, please don't waste time; look at the poems and forgive us our rhymes.

MORE POETRY NEWS

Salem poet Nancy Gordon will present a series of thematically linked and powerfully personal poems entitled *Dancing With Yang* on Sunday, April 28. This performance will feature live original music by Bryan Bridges, Salem, on didgereedoo and percussion, and Bart Walsh, Portland, on saxophone and flute. Dance will be performed by Willamette freshman Jenni Updenkelder. This performance will be held in the Hatfield Room of the library at 7 p.m. Call x2973 for more information.

OTHER

THROUGH APRIL 30

The ACLU Foundation of Oregon's traveling photo-journal exhibit, *Faces of Liberty*, is on display at the Mark O. Hatfield Library. A set of nine panels document, through black and white photographs and text, eight stories of Oregonians who stood up for basic civil rights. x6312.

ANNOUNCEMENTS
AND
INVITATIONS

AN INVITATION

The President of Lafayette College
and the
Friends of the Skillman Library
request the pleasure of your company
at a reception to view
"The Dixie Cup: An American Original"
Exhibition at Lafayette

Thursday, March 10, 1994
Skillman Library
4:30 to 6:00 p.m.

Special guests will be Louise Moore Pine
and officials of the James River Corporation.
RSVP by March 4

Marymount University
Arlington, Virginia

SELECTIONS FROM MEMBERS OF THE
WASHINGTON CALLIGRAPHERS GUILD
(including work by alumna Mary Delisio)

September 11 – October 31, 1995

OPENING RECEPTION
Friday, September 15
5:00-7:30 PM
Gallery Hours: M-Th 10-8, Fri. & Sat. 10-6
Phone: 703-522-5600

 Barry Gallery
Marymount University
Reinsch Library
2807 North Glebe Road
Arlington, VA 22207

Disabled access available to Reinsch Library

Selections
by members of
The Washington Calligraphers Guild

The Emerson College Alumni Club of Greater Boston
cordially invites you to

An Afternoon with Gilbert and Sullivan

Sunday, November 12, 1995   2PM - 5PM

Emerson College Library

150 Beacon Street Boston, Mass

View the extensive collection of Gilbert and Sullivan memorabilia
donated to Emerson College by Dr. Sigmund Lavine,
author and authority on Gilbert and Sullivan.

- Discuss the life and times of Gilbert and Sullivan
- Come to a reception honoring Dr. Sigmund Lavine
- Selections from the works of Gilbert and Sullivan
  will be performed

RSVP to the Office of Alumni Relations: (617) 578-8535.

Emerson College Library
Emerson College
Boston, Massachusetts

Swarthmore College
Swarthmore, Pennsylvania

SWARTHMORE COLLEGE LIBRARY
is pleased to present

Fine Printers Finely Bound Too

A Guild of Book Workers Exhibition
February 15 - March 15, 1994

Sponsored by
The Associates of the Swarthmore College Libraries.

Opening Reception Thursday, February 17, 1994 4:30 - 6:30

Hours:	Monday-Friday:	8:30 a.m. - 10:00 p.m.
	Saturday:	9:00 a.m. - 6:00 p.m.
	Sunday:	Noon - 10:00 p.m.

Front: Bicyclist, G. Delbruck/1890/French/Chromolithogragh/Sally Fox Collection

You are cordially invited to attend
a reception for
"The Sporting Woman: InSights From Her Past"
an exhibition of historic pictures documenting
the history of women in sports.

Friday September 20   12:30 pm   Shain Library

Connecticut College

Curator/picture researcher **Sally Fox**
will give a talk entitled

**"Histories Denied, Histories Revealed--
Original Picture Research as a Tool to
Document and
Illuminate Women's Varied Pasts"**

at 1:00 pm in the Haines Room
Refreshments will be provided
Ms. Fox will be available for interviews

POSTERS

Lafayette College
Easton, Pennsylvania

Small Books

LARGE IMPACT

The miniature books and book collection of Jane Conneen

FALL 1995 EXHIBIT
SPECIAL COLLECTIONS READING ROOM
DAVID BISHOP SKILLMAN LIBRARY
SEPTEMBER-DECEMBER, 1995
10:00 A.M. TO 5:00 P.M. DAILY

LAFAYETTE: FREEDOM'S FAVORITE SON

Spring Exhibition in Honor of the
Bicentennial of the French Revolution

January 20 — June 3, 1989
Special Collections Reading Room
David Bishop Skillman Library
Lafayette College

1:00 - 5:00 p.m., Mon. - Fri., and 7:00 - 10:00 p.m., Sun. - Thurs.
or by appointment
Support for this exhibition was provided by
William W. Lanigan '52

FROM NAST TO TRUDEAU

One Hundred Years of American Political Cartoons

1990 Spring Exhibition in Honor of the Comic Spirit Symposium

FEBRUARY - JUNE, 1990

Special Collections Reading Room
David Bishop Skillman Library

1:00 P.M. - 5:00 P.M., Mon. - Fri.
or by appointment

LAFAYETTE COLLEGE

THE CRADLE OF LIBERTY IN DANGER.
"Fee-Fi-Fo-Fum!" The Genie of Massachusetts smells Blue Blood.

BOOKLETS

[excerpts]

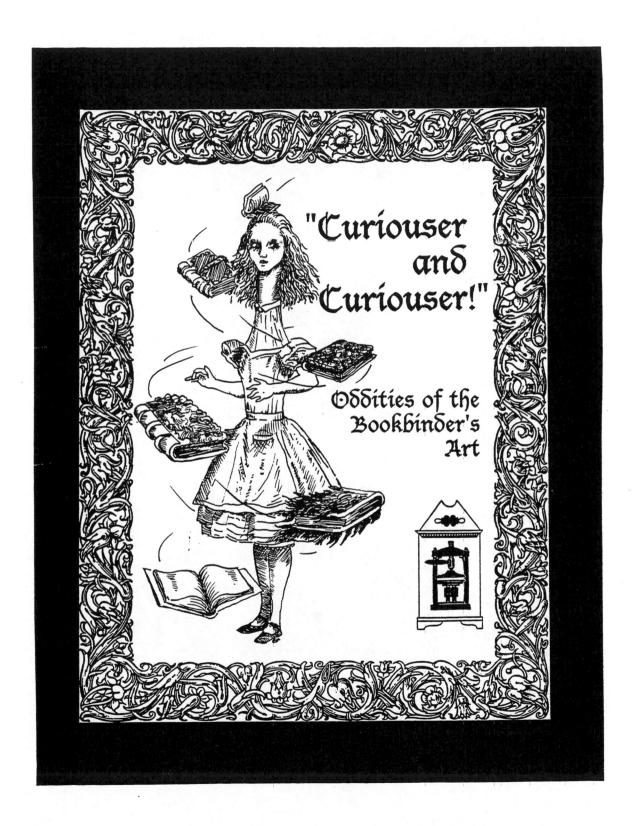

Occidental College
Los Angeles, California

ROBINSON JEFFERS, POET

1887–1987

A Centennial Exhibition

BIBLIOGRAPHIES

[excerpts]

Knight-Capron Library
LYNCHBURG COLLEGE

APRIL 16-18, 1993

▼

THE SECOND
Celebration

Faculty Scholarship & Creativity

The Collection of

Lynchburg College Faculty Publications

and Creative Works

Includes The Works Of Current, Emeritus, And
Retired Faculty And Staff Members

In Appreciation to
Cover Design: Patricia Kiblingler
Text: Marjorie Freeman

Muhlenberg College
Allentown, Pennsylvania

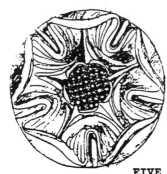

Harry C. Trexler Library

Muhlenberg College

Allentown, PA 18104

FIVE CENTURIES: THE MUHLENBERG COLLECTIONS

This exhibit contains items drawn from the Special Collections in the Harry C. Trexler Library. These collections are:

   The Muhlenberg College Collection consisting of over
       1600 faculty, alumni and college publications;
   The Pennsylvania German Collection consisting of over
       2000 items relating to the Pennsylvania German
       language, history and social customs, including
       a representative collection of 18th century German
       language imprints published in the United States;
   The Treasure Collection consisting of rare materials,
       first editions and autographed editions; and,
   The Abram Samuels Sheet Music Collection consisting
       of over 50,000 pieces of sheet music
       representing American popular music in the
       20th century.

FORERUNNERS OF THE PRINTED BOOK

   Babylonian cuneiform tablets. 2350-538 B.C.

   Oxyrhynchus Papyri. P. Oxy. 934. <u>Letter of Aurelius
       Stephanus.</u> (Manuscript) 3rd century A.D.

       A letter concerning domestic and agricultural
       purchases from Aurelius Stephanus to his brother.
       The bulk of the papyri found at Oxyrhychus in
       Egypt is housed in the Ashmolean Museum,
       Oxford University.

INCUNABULA (Books printed before 1500)

   Ovid. <u>Publii Ovidii Nasonis Epistolarum Herodium</u>. Venice:
       Baptista De Fortis, 1485.

       Appears to be the first edition of this work.

   Suetonius. <u>Caii Suetonii Tranquilli De Vita Duodicem
       Caesarum</u>. Venice: Bernard De Nouaria, 1491.
       Bound with: Valla, Lorenzo. <u>Elegantia Lingua Latina</u>.
       Venice: 1491.

Mothers and Others

Victorian Literary Association
Books, Drawings, and Letters
from the Collection of
MARK SAMUELS LASNER

•

Exhibited at the
Charles E. Shain Library
Connecticut College
22 September – 30 November
1995

· 3. AUBREY BEARDSLEY.
A Visitor at the Rehearsal.
Ink on paper, [1893].

For a period of months in 1893 the young and unknown Beardsley provided caricatures and comic sketches for *The Pall Mall Budget*, a weekly news magazine and gossip sheet. These drawings bear but slight resemblance to the artist's fully developed, instantly recognizable style found in the illustrations for Wilde's *Salome*. *A Visitor at the Rehearsal* portrays the distinguished actor Henry Irving. It appeared in the 16 March issue in an article, "Orpheus at the Lyceum," describing the production of Gluck's opera at the theater with which Irving (and his co-star Ellen Terry) were closely associated. Possibly once owned by Vyvyan Holland, Oscar Wilde's son, this drawing was later in the collection of David Joyce.

Occidental College
Los Angeles, California

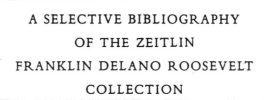

A SELECTIVE BIBLIOGRAPHY
OF THE ZEITLIN
FRANKLIN DELANO ROOSEVELT
COLLECTION
by
MICHAEL C. SUTHERLAND
with a preface by
LAWRENCE CLARK POWELL

A Keepsake for the May 11th Dinner Meeting
of the Library Patrons of Occidental College
and the dedication of
The Franklin Delano Roosevelt Collection
given in memory of Jacob I. ("Jake") Zeitlin
by Sam and Isabella Zeitlin

THE LIBRARY PATRONS OF OCCIDENTAL COLLEGE
LOS ANGELES, CALIFORNIA
1988

Magale Library
Southern Arkansas University
Magnolia, Arkansas

MISCELLANEY

THE SEARCH FOR BURIED TREASURE

Purpose of contest: The purpose of this contest
is to familiarize students with basic library
resources. The "treasure" being searched for is
the knowledge that can be gained from developing
logical thinking patterns needed for library
research.

Contest Regulations: It is important that you
try to use specialized, as opposed to general,
resources (for example, an art encyclopedia
instead of the Encyclopedia Britannica). When
answering each question, indicate source used,
call number, and the page number the answer was
located on.

Judging will be based upon thoroughness of answers
and the variety of resources utilized.

Contest responses are due Monday, October 24. Winners will be announced on
Halloween (Monday, October 31).

Houghton Memorial Library
Huntingdon College
Montgomery, Alabama

Illinois Wesleyan University
Bloomington, Illinois

First Annual
University Libraries
Art Purchase Award

The *First Annual Sheean Library Art Purchase Award*
will be announced at the B. A. and B.F.A.
Exhibition Opening Reception on April 21, 1996.
The award will be chosen from senior art show entries
by the University Librarian in cooperation with the
faculty of the School of Art.
This award consists of a $300.00 Cash Prize.
In addition to the cash prize, the recipient will receive
a framed and matted certificate of award.
All current senior applicants for the B. A. and B.F.A. in
the School of Art are eligible to receive the award.
Work in any medium that can appropriately become
part of the library's visual environment and
permanent collection will be considered for the
award, the only restrictions being those of scale and
durability of material.

The chosen work will be prominently displayed in the
library for one year. Thereafter, the work will remain
a permanent piece of the library's collection. Each
work will be identified with the artist's name, the year
awarded, the work's title, and its medium.
If an artist wishes to withdraw their senior show
entries from consideration, the artist should notify the
Chair of the School of Art.

First Annual University Libraries
Art Purchase Award

Awarded to

CAROLINE A. SACHAY

PART OF A WHOLE
Oil on Canvas

Sunday, April 21, 1996

Sue Stroyan, University Librarian   Miles Bair, Director of the School of Art

Sheean Library
Illinois Wesleyan University
Bloomington, Illinois

Swisher Library and Learning Resource Center
Bethune-Cookman College
Daytona Beach, Florida

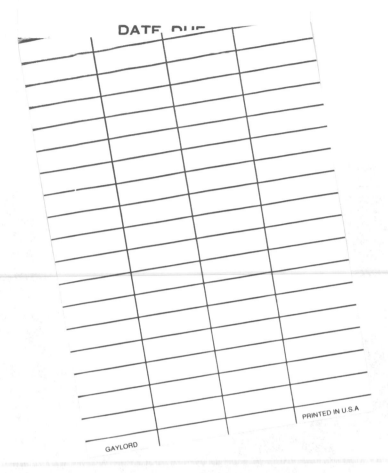

DATE DUE

GAYLORD

PRINTED IN U.S.A